COMMUNICATION – CRYSTAL CLEAR

How to CONNECT WITH YOUR CHILD

use your head …
and speak from the heart!

Order this book online at www.trafford.com
or email orders@trafford.com

Most Trafford titles are also available at major online book retailers.

Printed in the United States of America.

ISBN: 978-1-4120-7091-1 (sc)

 www.trafford.com

North America & international
toll-free: 1 888 232 4444 (USA & Canada)
phone: 250 383 6864 ♦ fax: 812 355 4082

COMMUNICATION – CRYSTAL CLEAR

How to CONNECT WITH YOUR CHILD

use your head …
and speak from the heart!

ROBIN TICIC

to Jesse,

for whom I began this journey

many years ago

ACKNOWLEDGMENTS

One of the nice side effects of writing a book is the opportunity to make public statements of gratitude.

Mountains of thanks go to my husband John for his steadfast, loving support and his complete acceptance of me as the person I am.

I thank my sons Zach, Jesse, Gustavo, and Jhon Alex for being my teachers. From them I have learned that my efforts to be a better mother have been worth the investment.

Much appreciation and respect are due the many people who, over the years, have trusted me to help them and have allowed me to share in their lives.

For helping to shape the convictions that govern my work and my life, I am indebted to the late Dr. Thomas Gordon, who crystallized some of the most important aspects of psychotherapy into a form appropriate for parents' use, and to Bruce Ecker and Laurel Hulley, for their work in the area of coherence therapy, a non-pathologizing approach to psychotherapy.

With regard to this book in particular, I thank John, Zach, and my sister Elise for working intensively with me, as well as Jesse, my sister Fern, my cousin Bert, my friends Jackie and Lori, and the people at Trafford for their contributions and support.

CONTENTS

INTRODUCTION: HOW TO BE THE BEST PARENT POSSIBLE

"Trying to get through to my kid is like talking to the wall!"

"Where do I draw the line when it comes to discipline?"

"We're always arguing about how to deal with our kids."

"I feel like the family slave! I have needs and desires, too."

Does any of this sound familiar to you? Are you tired of the conflicts and misunderstandings? As a mother of four boys, I know what this can feel like! But we're supposed to enjoy spending time with those who are most important to us, aren't we? So what can we do to set things on a better course? How would it be to have a step by step approach to improvement?

As both a parent and a psychologist, I've spent many years observing and analyzing what happens between parents and their children. Together we'll look at a wealth of real-life examples, examining patterns and habits of communication. We'll explore a proven method of finding your way through these sorts of dilemmas. You, like many parents I've had the privilege of working with before you, will find more clarity when dealing with typical "problem situations" as well as everyday interactions in the family.

When your son refuses to do his homework, for instance, or your daughter won't clean up her room, what can you do about it? We'll be looking at ways of resolving dilemmas like these. You'll learn methods that you can use to generalize from one specific situation to others systematically, once you understand their similarities. It's like having a master cookbook that's so clear and so thorough that you can create practically any recipe you need!

You'll find yourself becoming more relaxed as a parent. Problems won't seem so overwhelming, because you'll have a much better idea how to deal with them. Parenting will be more rewarding and less stressful. The ways that you and your children communicate with one another will become more constructive. So get ready! We're in for a wonderful adventure together.

LAYING THE FOUNDATION

1. FEELING FRUSTRATED?

Welcome to parenthood! You've already taken the first step toward making things better: you recognize that something is amiss. It's absolutely normal to experience complications in family life. It's guaranteed. What's important is *how* you deal with the complications when they arise. Can you do it in a way that improves the relationship you have with your child?

There's a nice thing about problems: you almost always get another chance (and another and another ...) to do things differently. The difficulties that crop up in families tend to recur. Otherwise you probably wouldn't view them as difficulties in the first place.

How to get the most out of this book

There will be many suggestions for practical exercises throughout this book. The more you make use of such opportunities, the more you and your children can benefit. There will be no "right" or "wrong" answers. What's right for one individual isn't necessarily right for another.

The ideas I present to you in this book have worked well for me and many other parents. Give them a good try, and then make your own decisions about what helps you.

How do you know if someone has a problem?

Let's say you have a feeling that something is bothering your child. What are some of the signs that point you in that direction? Many times we have no clue as to what is amiss, but we notice that something just isn't right. Take a few minutes now to note all the possibilities that might tip you off. For instance, if your child is usually very talkative and suddenly becomes very quiet, that could indicate a problem. Bear in mind that a "problem" can be anything from a mild disturbance to something really big.

How I notice that my child is bothered by something:

1.

2.

3.

4.

5.

...

...

...

Here are some signs that a child may be disturbed about something:

body language:
stooped posture, moving more slowly than usual
facial expressions:
looking sad, worried, scared, distracted
mental capabilities:
difficulty concentrating, trouble remembering
emotions:
aggression, withdrawal, sadness, anxiety, irritability
physical signs:
changes in sleep patterns, changes in toileting
verbal communication:
less or more than usual, louder or quieter than normal

What about the situation where there doesn't seem to be anything bothering your child, but you find that you yourself are disturbed by something? There are often early warning signs, even before you know exactly what's disturbing you. Jot down the changes you might notice in yourself when a difficult situation is brewing.

How I notice that I am bothered by something:

1.

2.

3.

4.

5.

...

...

...

Here are things I sometimes notice about myself when something is bothering me: I have less patience than usual, a decreased ability to concentrate, a tendency to become less diplomatic than I know I should be, or I'm more likely to be frustrated by small things. A friend of mine says she sometimes notices "a feeling of non-specific impending doom" when something is bothering her. Each person has somewhat different tendencies in general, and doing exercises like these can help us recognize signals of our own particular "hot button" areas. The specifics of the situation play a role, too, of course. For example, rainy weather is less likely to bother me if I'm working in the office than when I have my heart set on doing something outdoors. Simply being aware of such differences can be a first step toward minimizing difficulties.

What's the problem?

We have now looked at what we might notice when a person has a problem. That person might be our child, or our self, or maybe both of us are experiencing difficulties. What is it that actually happens – or doesn't happen – that leads to that state?

Please take a few moments to think about an actual problem you've had. Was there something you needed but didn't have? Or did you want something that wasn't forthcoming? That "something" isn't limited to tangible or material items. It could be the sleep you need when you're dead tired, or the good listener you're wishing for when you've had a terrible day.

Now think about a time your child had a problem. What was it that was lacking? Was something standing in the way of the child getting what she needed or wanted? Maybe your child was hungry and the food wasn't ready yet. Perhaps most of the neighborhood children were away and there weren't any playmates.

I have more clarity about myself when I can differentiate, for example, between my running low on patience (an indication that something is amiss with me) and the realization that I haven't had a decent meal in many hours (a basic need of mine isn't being met). I like to conceptualize a problem as *a situation in which a person's needs or desires are not being met*. Think about a specific experience you've had where you felt uncomfortable. Then try out this description of "problem" – a situation in which your needs or desires aren't being met – and see how well this definition fits.

Basic needs

Here's another useful exercise: make a list of all the different types of needs that occur to you. Then jot down whether you think each is relevant to children, to adults, or to both. For example, we need nourishment. We also need to socialize. (Granted, people differ on this score!)

needs:	*children?*	*adults?*
1. nourishment	x	x
2. socializing	x	x
3.		
4.		
5.		
6.		
7.		

8.

9.

10.

...

...

...

...

...

I wonder if you've discovered something that many of the participants in my parenting classes have seen: parents and children really do have a lot in common when it comes to basic needs. Of course, they don't always have the same need at the same time, as when a baby wants to play at 4 A.M. and the parents want to sleep. That's when conflicts materialize.

A lot has been written on the topic of universal human needs and the idea that there are generally priorities when it comes to satisfying needs. (Probably the most well-known model was developed by Abraham Maslow.) For instance, there are basic biological requirements for sustaining life, like water and food, sleep, air. What happens to other needs when an absolutely life-critical need isn't being met? The others tend to fade into the background. If you can't breathe, you won't be thinking about much else!

Only when those vital needs are satisfied is it usual for people to be concerned about the next level, which is very important but not as immediately critical: safety – with regard to one's body, family, home. Thinking in this way makes it easy to understand why someone would risk his safety to obtain food, for example.

A further category is that of love, belonging, acceptance. Again, it is generally the case that the previous levels need to be in order before attention can be given to this next (less urgent) area. When a family environment is abusive, for example, a child cannot develop feelings of being loved and accepted. Here's a different sort of example, but it illustrates the same point. My husband and I were in an amusement park, on one of the rides. It was a huge structure that swung back and forth, gathering more and more momentum until it felt as if all of us would swing over the top and go flying. Suddenly I became very frightened, and began thinking I was about to die. My husband, trying to comfort me, told me that he loved me. I screamed back at him at the top of my lungs, "I don't *care!*" (Actually, I was even more graphic than that.) Right then, believing my safety was on the line, his message of love was totally irrelevant to me!

Let's take this whole concept one step further: if a little girl hasn't had the experience of being loved and accepted the way she is, how can she develop self-esteem and self-respect (yet a further level of human need)?

Here's a way of looking at the four categories just described:

4. *self*-respect
3. love, *belonging*, acceptance
2. *safety*, security (body, family, home)
1. biological requirements for *staying alive*

I find it constructive to use a model like this when considering people and their problems. We sometimes find that the most visible "problem" is actually a result of needs not being met at a more basic level. A child who fears for his bodily safety in the schoolyard may stop caring about how well he performs in the classroom. A child who steals, even though he knows it's wrong, may be lacking something much more fundamental than moral conviction.

Generalized models of this sort help us grasp "the big picture." It's equally important to keep in mind, though, that people are unique. We're all different, even when it comes to needs as basic as sleep and food. Some people can get along just fine on five hours of sleep a night, for instance, whereas most others need significantly more.

Parenting goals

How is the topic of human needs related to our goals as parents? And what are our goals, anyhow? Of course we want our children to be happy, productive, law-abiding, and so on. The list could be almost endless. Please take a moment now to note the most important goals you, as a parent, have for your children.

What I want for my children:

    1.

    2.

    3.

    4.

    5.

    ...

    ...

    ...

When I think in terms of need fulfillment, I come up with something pretty simple and straightforward as my goal for my children: I hope they will be able to fulfill their own needs and desires and, at the same time, respect other people's right to do the same. I hope this will be a useful framework for you, too.

Clear communication

We began this chapter with the question, "Feeling frustrated?" When there are no problems between us and another person, it's usually not of critical importance to think about how to communicate with that person. It just flows naturally. When there's some difficulty, though, it can be a huge help to examine our ways of talking and listening.

How effectively are we communicating with our children? What does "effective" mean? So many times, a person says and means one thing – and the other person understands something quite different from what was intended. Sometimes it's as if they don't even speak the same language! We can define "effective communication," then, to mean that the message intended by the "sender" of the message is the same as what is understood by the "receiver" of the message. Although this isn't totally possible, since the sender and the receiver are two different individuals, we can do a lot to approach that goal.

For us as parents, this definition works in two directions. On one hand, we want to be able to communicate clearly to our children, so they understand what we mean. On the other hand, we also need to be receptive to our children in a way that enables them to communicate their thoughts and feelings to us. The first category can be thought of as *giving* information, the second as *receiving* information. These two categories of skills will constitute the bulk of our journey together throughout this book.

A frame of reference

Over the years I have dealt with countless situations where something has gone wrong in the communication between people. After the fact, it's often possible to analyze *what* actually happened and *where* something went awry. The ultimate goal, though, is to recognize what's happening *as it happens*, rather than afterwards. That way it's possible to get things back on track right away. In order to assist myself and, therefore, other people in pursuing this goal, it has been useful to me to work with a theoretical framework that I call the "Communications Matrix©." The matrix helps us see certain things with great clarity. Is it exciting? You bet!

2. THE COMMUNICATIONS MATRIX

In this chapter we will begin working with the Communications Matrix. In a mathematical sense, a matrix is an arrangement of rows and columns, but don't let that intimidate you. According to the first of many definitions in Webster's Unabridged Dictionary, a matrix is "that which gives origin or form to a thing or which serves to enclose it." This ability to lend form will be the characteristic most useful to us. Our model helps with those confusing sorts of interpersonal situations that seem to get out of hand so quickly that we're left asking ourselves afterwards, "Hey, what just went wrong here?" We'll go through many such examples throughout this book.

Our goal is a journey that I hope will continue for you long after you finish reading this book. For me, the skills involved in effective communication are a lifelong project, like so many other aspects of life where we strive to improve or become more knowledgeable. That means that I keep looking back and realizing how far I've come. I also look ahead and see that there's always room for improvement. Wherever I happen to be on this journey is okay, because I'm doing the best I can. This is a very empowering attitude that you can adopt, too. Sometimes the going gets rough, and you should take a moment then to pat yourself on the back. Why? Because you're interested in becoming an *even better* parent. Otherwise you wouldn't be reading this right now. And remember – children are great for giving you another chance!

Building the Communications Matrix

We'll be building the Communications Matrix step by step. The first part consists of a simple scale that looks like this:

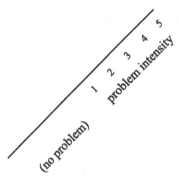

how bothered am I by this situation?

You'll understand shortly why this scale is pictured diagonally. We'll be using the values of 1 to 5 to rate how much *you yourself* are bothered by a particular problem situation. (We'll deal with the "other person" in a moment.) A value of 1 indicates being mildly disturbed, and 5 means severe disturbance. For instance, if you are trying to talk on the phone and your child starts playing and singing loudly in the same room, that will probably bother you. Maybe it's a really important call and you want to make a good impression. Or maybe you're just chatting with a friend and you feel free to say, "Hang on a minute while I deal with my kid." In the first instance, you'd most likely rate your level of disturbance higher than in the second case. Maybe you wouldn't be at all disturbed in the second situation. People and their reactions vary enormously. In addition, the same person can react differently from one time to the next, even if the situation is essentially the same. We all know that we have different tolerance levels at different times, depending on many factors, like how well we feel at that moment or whether we happen to have other problems on our mind.

The second piece of the matrix is essentially a mirror image of the first part and looks like this:

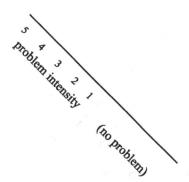

how bothered is my child by this situation?

We use this section to rate how much the *other person* involved in the problem (your child, for instance) is bothered by the situation in question. Again, we use a scale of 1 to 5. This breakdown is arbitrary but works well for most people. Let's continue with the example mentioned above. Maybe your child is having the time of his life while you're on the phone. We would place him in the "no problem" area of our scale, then, because he is not disturbed whatsoever by the current situation. Perhaps, though, he is tired, hungry, and running out of patience. We'd rate him reasonably high on the "problem intensity" scale then.

Now we can start to do something really interesting with these two pieces of the matrix by joining them together and then indicating *how disturbing* our problem situation is to *which people*. If we take the telephone call example and determine that your child is slightly annoyed that you're on the phone instead of paying attention to him, you might rate his disturbance level at 1. If you are having a serious conversation and find your child's noise very distracting, perhaps you find yourself at a level of 3.

The matrix now looks this way:

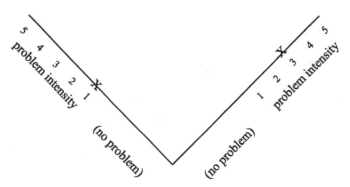

how bothered is my child by this situation?   how bothered am I by this situation?

My child is slightly annoyed
(disturbance level 1 out of 5)

I feel very distracted
(disturbance level 3 out of 5)

Now let's "combine" the two ratings:

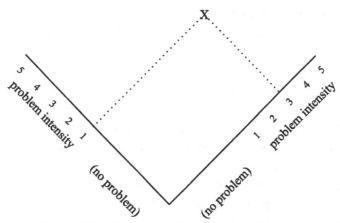

how bothered is my child by this situation?   how bothered am I by this situation?

My child is slightly annoyed
(disturbance level 1 out of 5)

I feel very distracted
(disturbance level 3 out of 5)

We now have a joint rating that shows both people's feelings in this situation. You may recognize this as a simple graph that has been rotated somewhat.

In another variation of the phone call situation, your child really needs something from you and is feeling upset. Let's estimate his level of disturbance at 3. You've been engrossed in a great conversation with your sister, and don't yet realize that your child is upset. For you the situation still feels unproblematic, so you're in the "no problem" area right now. The two ratings look like this:

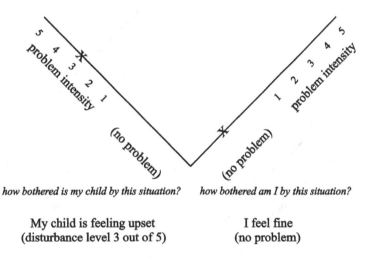

how bothered is my child by this situation?   *how bothered am I by this situation?*

My child is feeling upset   **I feel fine**
(disturbance level 3 out of 5)   **(no problem)**

When we combine the two points into a single image, as we did before, this is what we have:

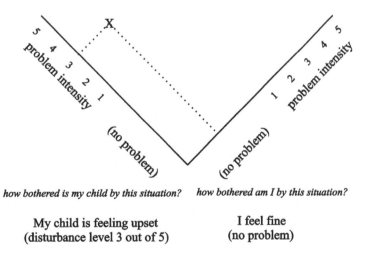

how bothered is my child by this situation?   *how bothered am I by this situation?*

My child is feeling upset   **I feel fine**
(disturbance level 3 out of 5)   **(no problem)**

Now, for clarity and usability, let's make the Communications Matrix fancier, more colorful, and much more versatile (after all, this book is about crystal clear communication!). Using the two scales we already have, we form an area that covers all ratings up through 5:

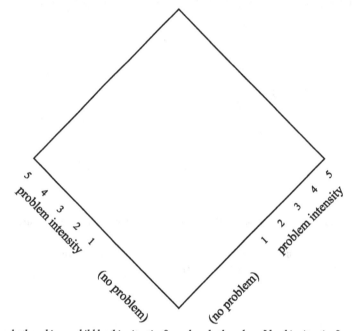

how bothered is my child by this situation?   *how bothered am I by this situation?*

We add some special color:

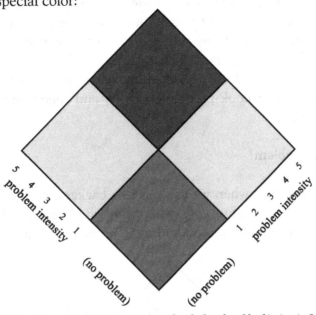

how bothered is my child by this situation?   *how bothered am I by this situation?*

and then descriptions of four different types of situations:

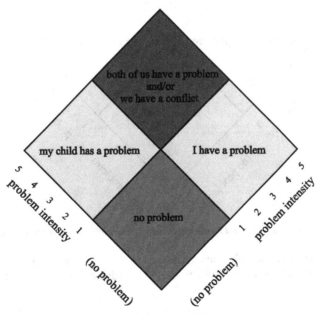

how bothered is my child by this situation?   *how bothered am I by this situation?*

Communications Matrix © Robin Ticic 2003, revised 2005

You can probably see now why I chose to view the matrix at this angle rather than in the more conventional horizontal-vertical position. This gives us a more balanced view of "my side" and the "other person's" side of things. I assume my choice of colors is clear to you, too! Take a good look at the colors now, because most of the remaining matrices are shown in shades of gray in order to keep book production costs, and therefore your purchase price, reasonable.

Who has the problem?

Watch what happens when we use this as a background for looking at our last two examples. In the first case, where your child was slightly bothered by your being on the phone but you had a big problem with the noise level, it looks this way:

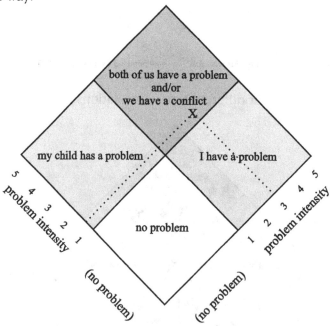

how bothered is my child by this situation?   how bothered am I by this situation?

My child is slightly annoyed
(disturbance level 1 out of 5)

I feel very distracted
(disturbance level 3 out of 5)

We automatically land in the section showing that, to varying degrees, "both of us have a problem" with this situation. In this example our needs are in conflict with one another. (There are also times when both people have a problem, but it's not a conflict between them. For example, it's a very hot night and everyone is having trouble sleeping.)

In the second example, where you are fine but your child is upset, this is what we have:

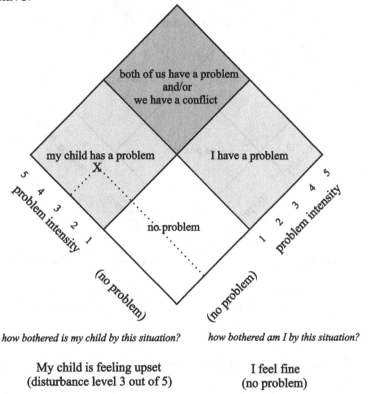

how bothered is my child by this situation?   *how bothered am I by this situation?*

My child is feeling upset   I feel fine
(disturbance level 3 out of 5)   (no problem)

We are in the section showing that "my child has a problem."

Yet another variation of the phone call scenario illustrates a different kind of situation. Your child is playing happily in her room. You have an important business matter to settle with the person on the phone, and the conversation drags on much longer than you'd expected. You're in a bind because you suspect, based on the sounds coming from your child's room, that she's destroying something. Look where we are in the Communications Matrix when we plot your child in the problem-free area and you at a disturbance level of 2, for instance:

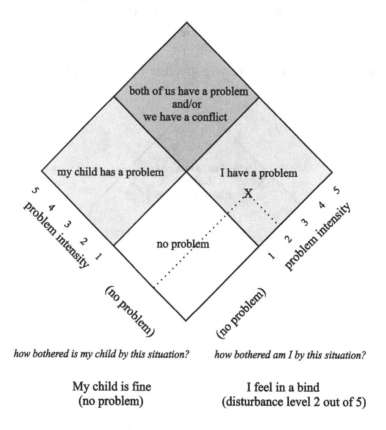

how bothered is my child by this situation?   how bothered am I by this situation?

My child is fine   **I feel in a bind**
(no problem)   **(disturbance level 2 out of 5)**

We are in the section showing that you are the one with the problem this time.

The breakdown into four sections is to some extent artificial. It's simple compared to real life, and for exactly that reason it's an excellent way of visualizing and clarifying what's happening in these situations, who is affected, and how much. As we progress, you'll see more and more how useful these four sections become.

Examples for practice

Here are several examples for you to work through by yourself. Again, there are no "correct" answers. I have left the descriptions very simple without indicating which person has what sorts of feelings. That way you can experiment with your own combinations of circumstances. Just use the Communications Matrix that follows, and enter the number of each of the ten examples at the location you think represents that particular situation.

1. Nine-year-old child's room is a mess.

2. Twelve-year-old is sick.

3. Seventeen-year-old has a failing grade on a test.

4. The kindergarten is closed for a week.

5. Fourteen-year-old has been "stood up" by her boyfriend.

6. Eight-year-old didn't come home from playing at agreed-upon time.

7. Ten-year-old has lied to parents.

8. It's time to eat but child doesn't come when called.

9. Teacher reports that child has misbehaved at school.

10. Six-year-old hits his twin brother.

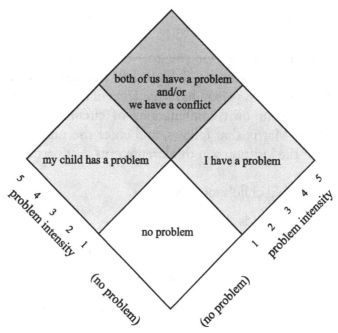

how bothered is my child by this situation?   *how bothered am I by this situation?*

In the following Communications Matrix, I've provided one possible answer for each of the above examples. Explanations for my ratings follow. Each answer is only one of many possibilities, depending on the particulars of each situation. What is important right now is for you to understand how to use the Communications Matrix.

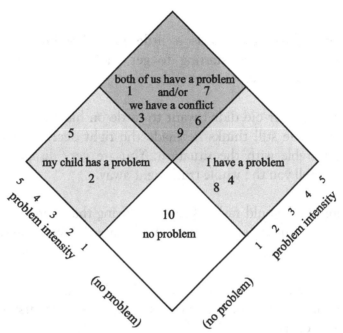

how bothered is my child by this situation?   how bothered am I by this situation?

1. Your nine-year-old is intent on playing and is furious that you're trying to get him to clean up his room. You have asked him several times, and you're getting aggravated.

2: Your twelve-year-old is at school and has started feeling ill. You don't yet know anything about it.

3. Your seventeen-year-old is very upset over the failing grade. You saw it coming and are displeased but not taken by surprise. You're hoping he learns from this.

4. Your child has no problem with staying home. You, on the other hand, are having difficulty lining up child care for the week so you can go to work.

5. For your fourteen-year-old this feels like the end of the world. You feel for her but realize that she will get over it and learn something from the experience.

6. Your eight-year-old feels a little bit guilty but was having fun playing. You were starting to get really worried when he didn't show up at home.

7. Your ten-year-old didn't want to tattle on his friend, so he made up a story. He still thinks he made the right decision but isn't totally comfortable with the situation. You are very disappointed that he didn't tell you the whole truth right away.

8. Your child would rather keep on playing than come to the table for lunch. You are in a hurry because you have an appointment soon.

9. Your child is afraid he'll be punished for misbehaving at school. You feel uncomfortable because this was your first contact with the teacher.

10. Your six-year-old feels he was justified in hitting his brother. You are confident they'll work things out with each other.

As you see in this last example, there are often more than just you and the "other person" involved in a problem. For the time being, though, to keep things as simple as possible, we'll be addressing mainly two-person situations.

Individual and situational factors

There are countless reasons that people react the way they do. Some reasons have to do with those *individuals* themselves, some have to do with *other people* who might be involved in a given situation, and yet other reasons have to do with the particulars of the *situation*.

We've already talked about how our tolerance levels are lower when we are ill, tired, or otherwise under stress. Those are factors that differ from time to time for any given individual. How about an example that has to do with the "other person": your two-year-old starts giggling with spinach in her mouth and dribbles it onto the table. Would you react differently if your ten-year-old did the same thing? We usually have different standards and expectations (which may or may not be reasonable!) for different people. The situation itself can also make a big difference in how much something bothers us. For instance, you stumble over something on the kitchen floor but catch yourself rather than falling. Would you feel the same way if you had been walking across the stage to give a presentation to a hundred people when you stumbled?

Here are some variables that contribute to my own reactions to people and situations:

1. Whether I've had a chance recently to do something for myself as opposed to having been "on call" for others all day: when I feel that I'm taking good care of myself, I have more tolerance in general for things going awry.

2. Whether a person who has a different set of ethical standards from mine is a close friend or only an acquaintance: I can deal much more easily with basic differences of opinion when I don't share my daily existence with the other person.

3. Whether I am with my family or with a client: I am better able to remain objective rather than becoming emotionally involved in the other person's problem when my relationship with that person is purely professional.

In each case, it's easy to see how I could be more accepting of a problematic situation under some circumstances than others.

Please take a few minutes to make your own individual list of factors that make a difference in how you react to a given situation.

Factors that may influence my reactions in a difficult situation:

1.

2.

3.

4.

5.

...

...

...

Now list those factors that you believe affect your child's ability to cope with problem situations.

Factors that may influence my child's reactions in a given situation:

1.

2.

3.

4.

5.

...

...

...

In this chapter we have laid the groundwork for working with the Communications Matrix. Next we will look in detail at one particular section of the matrix.

BUILDING UP A POSITIVE RELATIONSHIP

3. WHAT'S GREAT ABOUT GREEN?

I wanted to name this chapter "Theory, Philosophy, and History" but I thought it might sound too academic and that people might skip it. But since you're still reading, you'll see how vitally important these topics are. We're going to look at the green area of the Communications Matrix for a while. That's the part representing a more or less problem-free state. You may be asking yourself, "Why bother with that?" since you're reading this book to help you solve problems. Well, that's exactly the purpose of this book, and I will show you how to get back into the green area when you find yourself spending time in the yellow or red zones with your children.

First, though (and here comes the *Theory* part ...), I want you to understand what is so important about spending as much time as possible in the problem-free area with your children. There are many reasons.

Developing self-esteem

Being in the green area means that you feel accepting of your child and your child's behavior at present. Children develop positive feelings about themselves when they feel accepted by their parents. Imagine what it means to a child to spend most of his time feeling approved of by his parents. He grows up thinking – and feeling – that he's a pretty good person. I see a lot of people who land in therapy precisely because their parents were unable to do this for them.

Self-esteem grows when children's efforts and accomplishments are valued by their parents. When we're in the midst of dealing with problems, we're unlikely to say something like, "I really like that picture you drew. I can see you put a lot of work into it," or "I bet you're really proud of yourself." Staying in the green area lets you pay more attention to the positive aspects of life. Children – and their parents – benefit from that.

Changing oneself for the better

There's another important reason to spend as much of the time as possible in the green area with your kids. This will probably sound contradictory to you ... but the biggest prerequisite for a person improving himself is for that person to feel accepted and valued the way he is. Therapists experience this over and over again. In fact, the virtually unconditional acceptance a therapist can normally give a client is the very basis that enables that client to make significant changes. It's as though the person doesn't need to expend energy on defending how he is, and can funnel that energy in more constructive directions. The same goes for our children.

Talking about feelings

One of the most valuable skills we can teach our kids is the ability to recognize emotions and talk openly about them. Many people have difficulty doing this. It's especially challenging when the emotions are disapproved of or uncomfortable. When we're in the problem-free area with a child, it's much easier for both the parent and the child to talk about feelings than when things are hot with conflict. (It's like learning to ride a bike on a nice smooth road, rather than on one with stones and potholes.) This is a great way to get a child used to the idea that it's normal and desirable to talk about his feelings. Then when things get rough, the skills are already in place to deal with those uncomfortable feelings. This ability is a blessing for our children, the parents of the future.

Making it a habit

Here's another good reason for learning these skills when in the green zone. The experience of using these communications methods becomes linked up in our minds with the feelings of being in a positive situation. An inner voice says, "I feel good – I'm using these methods – I feel good – I'm using these methods – I feel good" and so on.

Recognizing problems sooner

When we get used to spending more time in the problem-free region (the green area of our matrix), we become more keenly aware of "crossing the border" into a problem area (yellow or red in the matrix). We become more sensitive to the signs that we're feeling uneasy, or that another person is experiencing a problem, or that a conflict is brewing. When danger signs are recognized early on, it's much easier to get back into the green zone than when things have really escalated.

Instead of this:

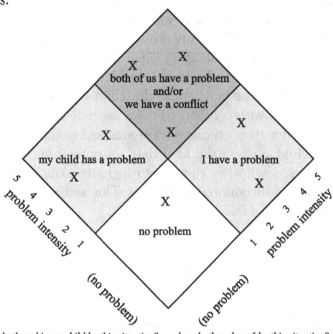

how bothered is my child by this situation?   how bothered am I by this situation?

we'll see more of this:

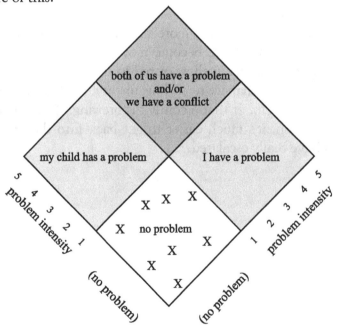

how bothered is my child by this situation?   how bothered am I by this situation?

Improving relationships

When someone experiences a relationship in a positive way, the relationship gets better. The relationship becomes linked in the person's mind with pleasure rather than discomfort. It's a self-perpetuating process. (How often have we seen the negative version of this process, where frequent conflicts send the relationship into a downward spiral?) And here's a big bonus: the better the relationship, the more incentive there is to understand the other person and cooperate with him. It's a no-lose ripple effect.

I remember one mother who came to me for help because she felt she'd almost completely lost contact with her teenage son. She decided to attend one of my courses. After about half the sessions, she reported that her son had really started to open up, and that he actively sought out her company. He'd begun talking to her about important parts of his life. And – up to that point in the course we had worked only in the problem-free area!

Enough for Theory; now how about a little bit of my personal *Philosophy*?

Helping the world's people

I look around the world and cringe at the violence and lack of understanding that afflict such a large part of this planet's people. I ask myself what can be done and, specifically, what I can do. My conviction is that genuine communication, along with the mutual understanding that results from that communication, is the basis for improvement. What better place to start than with our children, enabling them to interact in a healthier way with others and, later, with their partners and children? Only then will real caring and understanding spread from families to communities, from communities to nations, from nations to the world at large. We can reverse the vicious cycle of fear, resentment, hatred, and violence, not to mention the aftermath of alarmingly high divorce rates, by starting where we have the most influence – in our role as parents. Perhaps this strikes you as idealistic, and it's certainly a long-term project, but every effort helps.

And now for some *History*.

During the early period of using the matrix to teach communications skills to groups of people, my teaching partner and I assumed that conflict situations (the red area) would be the most difficult. After all, that's the time each person is looking out for his own interests without necessarily being very motivated to understand the other person's viewpoint, and tempers flare easily. Well, we made an exciting discovery. We found out that if we spent enough time practicing in the non-conflict problem areas (the yellow zones), mastering the skills needed when *only one person* has a problem, the conflict situations were almost a snap! In other words, learning to operate well in the yellow parts of the matrix really paves the way for knowing what to do in the red zone.

The next discovery was at least as significant. In teaching parents about communicating constructively with their children, I saw that the best time for learning the very basics is when they're in the green zone. That's not the entirety of the learning process but it's certainly the bulk. Then the skills needed in the yellow areas are already well in place. Do people learn first aid best in the midst of an emergency? Usually not.

Now you see why I want to teach you as much as possible about using healthy communications skills *when you're not having any problems with your children!* It will help *keep you* in that problem-free area. And that, after all, is our goal. It is very important to me that you understand my reasons for doing things in that order. In the next two chapters we'll see how to maximize the time you and your child spend in the green zone.

4. WHAT IS YOUR CHILD TELLING YOU?

What some of them are saying

What do *kids think their parents should do differently* to be better parents? The feedback from a survey I did with teenagers on this topic was fascinating. In the gender combination "fathers / daughters" the relationships overall received the worst ratings. And the biggest complaint these teenage girls had was "I can't talk to my father about my feelings." For a brief period I lamented that most readers of books about communication and child rearing are mothers, when fathers need these listening skills at least as much. Then my optimism got the better of me, and I realized that mothers can accomplish exactly what is needed by teaching their children – especially their sons – how to listen. In addition to the immediate benefits, these boys will grow up to be better parents (and better partners). Don't think I have something against males! I adore them, and have the privilege of sharing my life with several of them. It seems, though, that males – in general – seem to have less need to talk about feelings than do females. It's natural, then, that they sometimes show less interest in emotions than their partners or children would like.

After surveying teenagers, I thought it would be informative to ask *adults what their own parents could have done better.* Here's what I discovered. Out of sixteen categories that were rated, women judged both parents and men judged their fathers most harshly in exactly the same area as the teenage girls judged their fathers to be lacking: *listening skills!*

I have often wondered what the most important factors are that lead to good, healthy relationships between parents and their children. After questioning *parents who have very positive interactions with their children*, I began hearing some of the same things over and over again: "If your child wants to talk, then listen!" "Listen without judging!" "Listen without interrupting!" "Listen with respect!" "Listen to the kid's needs, not only your own!" These were the same parents who told me how important it is to have fun together, to go to the effort of letting children know about the good things they do, not just the "bad" things, and to give children the attention they need even when they're "behaving themselves," so they don't have to get it through negative channels.

We'll come back to more survey results in later chapters (and in Appendix 3 you can find more detailed information about the survey). The rest of this chapter is devoted to the idea of improving our listening skills when we are in the problem-free area with our children.

Supportive understanding

"Following ahead"

In therapy we sometimes use the motto, "Follow the client a little bit ahead." What a strange idea! We try to get on the client's wavelength by sensing what he or she is feeling. That's the "following" part. Then we can work with that by calling those feelings to the person's conscious attention and helping the client to verbalize those feelings. During that part we're "a little bit ahead." The client leads the way, but we give support with the message "I see where you are. I'd like to help you get a little bit further." Although we are not our children's therapists, this attitude is beneficial in raising children and is a good description of the skill I call "supportive understanding."

"Active listening"

This type of skill is often referred to as "active listening." "Supportive understanding" is the description that I prefer, for a couple of reasons. First of all, I've found that the word "active" sometimes misleads people into taking too much of a directive role (active *persuasion*), rather than "following a little bit ahead" (active *listening*). Secondly, "listening" is only part of what's needed to understand and support someone. We need to observe the person on various levels and really *feel* with the person. "Feeling with the person" means that you are able to empathize, to imagine how that person feels (which is different from having those same feelings yourself.) Our body language and facial expressions, and our physical interactions with that person are all part of this support.

A special kind of mirroring

Supportive understanding lets a child know you're on his wavelength, that you have an idea what's going on with him at the moment. This is a skill that becomes critically important when you find yourself in the yellow region where your child is having a problem. For now we'll be learning how to use this skill while still in the problem-free region.

The idea here is to function as a type of mirror that observes, processes, reformulates, and communicates back to the child to verify that the "mirror" has understood correctly.

Examples

For instance, it's mealtime and you notice that your child is eating with gusto. You say, "You're really enjoying eating those fresh peaches!" Your child grins. Let's have a look at exactly what's involved in this seemingly trivial comment. First you noticed that your child was happy, then you made an educated guess as to what triggered that happiness, then you "mirrored" (or reflected) back to your child what it was that you noticed. The grin from your child was a confirmation that you were on the right track.

It's mealtime once again and you watch your child experimenting with different ways of using her knife for cutting broccoli. She settles on cutting lengthwise rather than across the broccoli stalk. You make eye contact with her, and remark, "I see it's easier for you to cut the broccoli that way." She nods. Again, let's see what happened. You noticed your child dealing with a challenge, then witnessed the practical result that materialized, then mirrored back your observation. The nod showed that your child agreed with what you said.

Here is a more formal breakdown of what we described in the first example.

situation:	child eating fresh peaches
result:	child is happy

Your comment reflects both the triggering situation ("eating those fresh peaches") and the result ("you're really enjoying"). The child feels noticed and understood.

We can do the same thing with the second example.

situation:	child is trying to cut broccoli
result:	child finds a method that works well

Your comment reflects the initial situation ("to cut the broccoli") and the result ("it's easier for you ... that way"). Again, the child feels noticed and understood. She sees that you're interested in her.

As you may have realized in looking at these two examples, sometimes there are emotions that result from a particular situation, and sometimes there are purely practical results. There can be both. (Maybe the little girl cutting the broccoli was proud of herself, in addition to having solved a practical dilemma.) Just to make things more complicated, there are other categories of responses, like thoughts, behavior, and bodily sensations. For now, though, we'll concentrate on the practical results, because they're easy to observe and talk about, and the emotions, because they're very important. Often the emotional components are the most significant, so it's worthwhile paying special attention to them. Many times we notice children's emotions first, before we know what triggered them, as in the first example.

Often it's easier to understand things in pictures rather than using only words. These are the images I like to use:

🎥   *video camera* for a factual description of the situation,

♥   *heart* for the feelings, and

↗   *arrows* for practical results.

The video camera reminds me to be as objective as possible when describing a situation. I ask myself, "What would a video camera record in this situation?"

See if these pictorial versions of the two examples are useful to you:

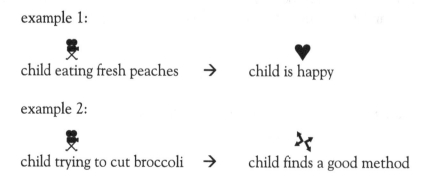

example 1:

🎥
child eating fresh peaches   →   ♥
                                   child is happy

example 2:

🎥
child trying to cut broccoli   →   ↗
                                     child finds a good method

As you see here, a given situation can cause an emotion to surface without any practical results being apparent, or it can be the other way around. In later examples we'll see other combinations.

Helping your child learn to notice and articulate emotions is an invaluable gift. The easiest time to get used to doing this is when the emotions are positive. In other words, do it when you're in the problem-free zone with your child. We don't necessarily think to operate this way when everything is going well, so that's why I'm drawing your attention to this idea.

To help out in describing positive feelings, here is a small list, with overlapping terms grouped together:

> ambitious, brave, calm, confident, enthusiastic, proud, trusting
> calm, cheerful, excited, happy, optimistic, relaxed, satisfied
> amazed, curious, interested, involved, fascinated, sympathetic
> accepting, admiring, affectionate, considerate, loving, understanding

Examples for practice

Some useful questions you can ask yourself as you're doing these exercises (and when you use this skill in real life) are:

- Are we really in the problem-free zone currently?
- What do I notice about my child's feelings right now?
- How can I describe those feelings?
- What situation might have led to the feelings?
- Is there some practical outcome to this situation that's of interest to my child?

Here are some exercises so you can practice formulating comments to show supportive understanding. Be careful that it's *your child's* feelings and situation that you're observing, and not your own (or those that you would like your child to have). Use your imagination about the particulars of each situation. I've left the descriptions very simple so you can experiment with different scenarios.

1. Six-year-old has received a party invitation from her best friend.

   ....

2. Ten-year-old gets a better grade than he expected on a math test.

   ....

3. Christmas is just a week away.

   ....

4. Four-year-old gets his first two-wheeler.

   ....

5. Daughter just passed her driver's test.

   ....

6. Seven-year-old goes to bed willingly because he's very tired.

   ....

Below are some possible responses for the examples. Remember, there aren't necessarily "correct" answers. Formulations can be as individual as the people who create them. The idea is to show interest and understanding.

1. "You seem really happy ♥ about that invitation!" ✗

2. "You're surprised ♥ that you got such a good grade on the math test. ✗ You're proud!" ♥

3. "You're so excited ♥ about Christmas ✗ that you can hardly sleep!" ⌁

4. "Wow! You feel like such a big boy ♥ now that you have a two-wheeler! ✗ You'll be able to ride around with the big kids." ⌁

5. "You're really proud ♥ to have a driver's license! ✗ Now you can come and go on your own." ✗

6. "You're so sleepy right now ✗ that you're going right to bed." ✗

Your child will let you know if you're on the wrong track. Let's look at example 5. Maybe your daughter hasn't even gotten to the stage of being proud yet, and you've misread her emotions. She might say, "Well, actually I'm just glad to have the test behind me. I'm so relieved that I passed!" Then you have the chance to get onto her wavelength and say something like "Yeah, it's a relief to have that over and done with!" Most likely she'd smile or nod in agreement, verifying that she feels understood.

Individual and situational factors

There are certain prerequisites for practicing supportive understanding. Since it is a way of showing someone that you're interested in him and are taking time for him, it is appropriate only when you really *are* interested and really *are* willing and able to spend the time on him. You can still be in the problem-free area with someone, and yet not be interested in what that person is doing at the moment. That's perfectly okay, and it's important to ask yourself where you stand on the questions of time and interest right then. Maybe you're concentrating on some personal bookkeeping and your child is working happily on a project nearby. Your attention is on what you're doing, and not necessarily on what your child is doing.

The other aspect to consider is whether your child is interested in such attention at the moment, or whether she'd rather just continue what she's doing. It might be more of an annoyance than a pleasure to your teenager if you interrupted her studying for an important test to comment on how hard she's working!

Practicing on your own

I suggest that you practice supportive understanding with each child a few times every day and just watch what happens. It's important to work on this skill in a non-problematic setting before moving on to the next steps. You can use the chart at the end of the chapter to note your experiences. (It's worthwhile to make some copies of the chart first, for future use.) Take the time you need to feel comfortable using supportive understanding. The more this skill becomes second nature during the good times, the more successful you'll be in using it when your child is having a problem. That's when it's of paramount importance.

It's normal to need lots of practice when learning a new skill. Just think back to learning how to drive, or playing a new sport. Give yourself as much encouragement as you can for having what it takes to try out something new. You'll reap rewards for your efforts, even when your efforts are less than perfect. Children notice that you're doing your best. Besides, your nonverbal communication will show your good intentions.

Some parents find it extremely difficult to interact with their children in this positive way. I recall a 36-year-old woman telling me that the thing she most would have liked her mother to do differently was "not to constantly criticize everything I talked about." If you feel resistant to the idea of being interested in your child, then please discuss this with a family counselor. Some parents find that there isn't really much of a problem-free zone in their relationship with a child. This can also indicate the need for professional support to get things on track.

In this chapter we've looked at how to let our children know that we're paying attention to them *even though* things are going well between them and us. Interacting this way with our kids is a very smart thing to do, because it encourages them to stay in the problem-free zone! They realize that *it isn't necessary to misbehave* to get attention from their parents!

In the next chapter we'll have a look at the other side of the coin: communicating with children to get them to pay attention to *us and our feelings – even though* we're in the problem-free area.

Work Sheet: **Supportive Understanding in the no-problem area**

date:

♟ situation:
♥ result (feelings):
✗ result (practical):

what I said:

how child reacted:

results, changes, etc.:

date:

♟ situation:
♥ result (feelings):
✗ result (practical):

what I said:

how child reacted:

results, changes, etc.:

date:

♟ situation:
♥ result (feelings):
✗ result (practical):

what I said:

how child reacted:

results, changes, etc.:

5. WHAT ARE YOU TELLING YOUR CHILD?

I-messages

I-messages let a child know what's going on with *you*. This skill is very useful when you land in the yellow region where you are having a problem. In this chapter, though, we'll start using this skill while still in the green area because, just as with supportive understanding, it's easier to learn a new skill when not distracted by problems. The format of this chapter is similar to that of the last one. This will help you see that I-messages and supportive understanding are really two sides of the same coin: promoting mutual understanding.

Why bother explaining to your child what you're thinking or how you're feeling, especially when there aren't any problems? This information gives your child the chance to get to know you better, and to learn what pleases you. This is more enjoyable for everyone than waiting until things get difficult and *then* letting the child hear what's bothering you. It helps you stay in the problem-free area. It often takes a conscious effort, though, to let someone know that we're pleased, whereas airing our gripes and grievances in great detail is usually something we do easily!

Let's use a mealtime example again. The family has finished breakfast, and your children clear the table. You say, "Wow! I'm really glad you guys cleaned up! Now I have time to sit and read the paper for a few minutes." You could have said simply "Thanks," which would have been fine. A well-formulated I-message, though, is much better, and here's why. You've pointed out how you feel ("really glad"), what practical implication the children's behavior has for you ("Now I have time to sit and read the paper for a few minutes"), and exactly what that behavior was ("you guys cleaned up"). You're giving them a lot of useful information!

Here's a formal breakdown of what happened.

situation:	children cleared the table after breakfast
results:	you are happy *and* you have time to read the paper

You may have noticed that this situation resulted in both an emotional response and a practical result. As with supportive understanding, the emotional components can be very important. By noticing and talking about your feelings, you're showing your children that it is acceptable to have feelings and to discuss them. You're being a good role model in that regard, even if your child has difficulty understanding your feelings. (You can look back at the short list of positive emotions in the last chapter if you need ideas for describing your feelings.) Practical results are often easier for children to comprehend than another person's emotions, so it's important to state them clearly, as well.

The pictorial version of our breakfast example looks like this.

kids cleared table   →   you're happy   *and*   have time to read

Examples for practice

The sorts of useful questions I listed in the last chapter with the exercises for supportive understanding are applicable here, too.

- Are we really in the problem-free zone currently?
- What do I notice about my feelings right now?
- How can I describe those feelings?
- What situation led to those feelings?
- Is there some practical outcome to this situation that's of interest to me?

Some exercises follow so you can try your hand at formulating I-messages.

1. Nine-year-old took out the trash without being asked.

    ....

2. Eleven-year-old twins played quietly together while parents worked on tax return.

    ....

3. Five-year-old went to bed without giving the babysitter much aggravation.

....

4. Twelve-year-old chose to drink juice rather than soda.

....

5. Seventeen-year-old cleaned up her room from top to bottom.

....

6. Son brought all his belongings back from a camping expedition.

....

7. Daughter called to say she'd be getting home later than expected, because the party's really fun.

....

Here are some possible answers for the above examples. Your answers might be just as good or better (and probably different!). It's very much up to the individual. The goal we have is to give our child information about us in a way the child can understand and use.

1. "I really appreciate ♥ your taking out the trash without me even needing to remind you! ✗ Now I can concentrate on getting dinner ready." ⤬

2. "I'm so glad ♥ we could get that paperwork done in a quiet atmosphere ✗. You two really cooperated! ✗ Now we have time to do something together." ⤬

3. "It's a nice feeling to know that <u>we can go out for a while</u> ✕ and <u>trust you</u> ♥ to be <u>good when the sitter is here</u>!" ✕

4. "<u>I'm proud</u> of you ♥ that <u>you chose a healthy drink</u>!" ✕

5. "Wow! <u>I'm impressed</u> ♥ by what a thorough <u>job you did</u>! ✕ <u>I like how your room looks</u> ♥ and now it's a lot <u>easier for me to put away your laundry</u>." ✕

6. "<u>I can really depend on you</u> to look after your belongings! ♥ <u>I feel good</u> about letting you take things on a trip ♥ when I know <u>you bring them all back</u>." ✕

7. "<u>I appreciate</u> ♥ <u>your letting us know</u> you'll be late. ✕ Now <u>I'll be able to finish reading</u> my book ✕ instead of being <u>worried</u> about you!" ♥

Individual and situational factors

Just as with supportive understanding, the circumstances have to lend themselves to using I-messages. You need to be interested in letting your child know what you're feeling; this is not always the case, and that's alright. In addition, your child needs to be receptive at that moment, otherwise the message gets lost. There are certainly times when you and your child are in the problem-free zone together but not interacting with one another because each is concentrating on something else.

Some tricky differences

There's something interesting and subtle about I-messages that I find important for you to know. Consider the difference between saying, for instance, "I like that picture you drew," as opposed to saying, "That's a nice picture." These two statements might strike you as being similar or interchangeable. The first statement describes your feeling. The second states a "fact." Suppose your child isn't satisfied with how the picture looks. She'd disagree that it's a nice picture, which is a matter of opinion, not fact. Your feeling about the picture, though, is something she can accept at face value without having to agree, because it's your feeling, not hers. Here's another example: there's a clear difference between "I'm proud of you!" and "You're a good girl." Your child may not feel like a good girl right then, but your feeling is simply your feeling. A good I-message conveys your emotion, rather than stating your opinion as if it were fact.

Sometimes it's a challenge to differentiate between supportive understanding and I-messages. Consider the statement, "Great! You've finished your homework. That's a relief!" Although this type of comment may be intended as supportive understanding, it's actually more of an I-message, because it emphasizes the parent's feelings more than those of the child. It's important to be clear about whose feelings you want to describe.

Practicing on your own

Please take the opportunity every day to practice I-messages with each child during a time when things are going well. The chart at the end of the chapter, which is the same as in the previous chapter, can be used to record your experiences now, in the problem-free zone. (You may want to make some copies, as suggested earlier.) You might even discover something new about yourself. Try using I-messages to tell your child something about you even when it has nothing to do with your child directly. "Today I ran into a woman who was in my class in grade school! It was so exciting to catch up with each other after all these years!" might very well be of interest to your child.

Ask yourself whether your nonverbal messages to your child are consistent with your verbal messages. Do your real feelings match what you're saying? In order to let someone else know how you feel, you have to know yourself well enough to be in touch with your own feelings first. Practice enough to become comfortable interacting with your child in this way. Then when you're in a situation where you're bothered about something, it will be that much easier to use I-messages.

It has been my experience that parents often find it easier to formulate I-messages than to use supportive understanding. Whichever way it turns out for you, try to enjoy the process and explore the possibilities, rather than expecting perfect results. Every small change will bring you further on your journey. Every little step will bring you closer to your children.

As I pointed out in the last chapter, if you really can't talk about positive things with your child, or if you find that things between you and your child are hardly ever in the problem-free area, please look for an appropriate professional to give you support and guidance.

We have now seen how to draw a child's attention to us *even though* everything is fine. The child feels encouraged to repeat those behaviors that please us, and that maximizes the time we spend in the problem-free area with our children. They get messages about what they're doing right, and not only messages about what they've done wrong! It is one of our important responsibilities as parents to seek out – *actively* – ways to stay in the problem-free zone with our kids.

The matrix

Let's just look at the matrix from a slightly different viewpoint for a moment. What are our responsibilities in each section? In the problem-free area, our job is to stay there, to strengthen the positive aspects of the relationship with our child.

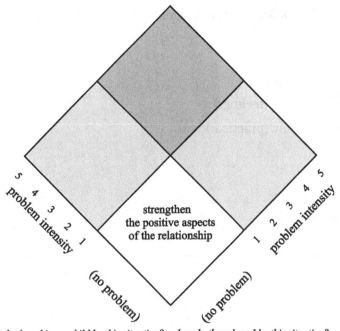

how bothered is my child by this situation?   how bothered am I by this situation?

As we move through the rest of this book, we'll address the question of responsibilities in the remaining three areas.

So far, we've worked on skills of supportive understanding and I-messages in the green zone. In the next section we'll see what to do when we cross the border over into the yellow area where your child is having a problem.

Work Sheet: I-messages in the no-problem area

date:

 situation:

 result (feelings):

result (practical):

what I said:

how child reacted:

results, changes, etc.:

---

date:

 situation:

result (feelings):

result (practical):

what I said:

how child reacted:

results, changes, etc.:

---

date:

 situation:

result (feelings):

result (practical):

what I said:

how child reacted:

results, changes, etc.:

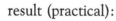

my child has a problem

HOW TO HELP YOUR CHILD WITH PROBLEMS

---

6. WHY LISTEN IF YOUR CHILD HAS A PROBLEM?

Parental goals

It's time to look again at the parenting goal I proposed in Chapter 1 when thinking about my own children: "I hope they will be able to fulfill their own needs and desires and, at the same time, respect other people's right to do the same." The best way to help children achieve the first part of this goal, fulfilling their own needs and desires, is to provide them with just the right amount of support and guidance. "Just the right amount" means supporting and guiding to the point where they are able to take on responsibility themselves. Of course that differs from one child to the next, and varies according to the situation. Specifically, I want my children to be active in taking on responsibility for solving their own difficulties. I want to provide them with what they need, and then let them loose. (By the way, parents vary significantly in how eager or reluctant they are for their children to become independent. Investigating this complex and challenging topic can help us understand ourselves better.) The second part of the goal, respecting other people's right to fulfill their needs and desires, is a topic in the next section of this book.

I try to view problems as opportunities for growth. The word "problem" itself implies moving ahead (from the Greek *pro*, meaning "forward"). Let's use our children's problem situations to help them take active control of their existences and learn to be self-reliant and self-confident. Interestingly, the Chinese word for "problem" has two meanings: difficulty and opportunity. *Difficulties* are *opportunities*.

So what is it that children need to solve their problems? Well, sometimes all that's needed is some information. "Mom, how many centimeters are there in an inch?" is pretty straightforward, assuming you know the answer. There aren't necessarily any strong feelings involved when there's a problem to solve. Sometimes it's simply a practical issue. There are other times, though, when emotions play a central role. Being shoved is easier to ignore when a child knows it happened by accident than when it's because his best friend is angry at him. These situations that involve emotions are the types we'll be looking at in this section of the book and this section of the matrix.

You'll discover that the emotions often play such a key role that once they've been addressed, the practical level of solving the problem is a piece of cake. Take the example of a child going to school for the first time. She's apprehensive, which is normal in a new situation. After her feelings of uncertainty have been talked through, accepted, and "normalized" by her parents (using supportive understanding), she trots off feeling self-confident enough to join the other children. The "problem" has been solved, even though the circumstances haven't changed. What the child needed was emotional support and understanding for her feelings.

As you may well know, differentiating between the need for emotional support and the need for practical support is a particularly valuable skill in couple relationships. Both men and women often feel totally misunderstood when the woman wants emotional support and the man offers practical solutions to her "problem." She doesn't feel understood and he doesn't feel appreciated. But that's a different topic for a different book! It's useful, though, to consider possible male-female differences when dealing with children, since these gender differences don't simply "appear" all of a sudden at the onset of adulthood.

Dealing with emotions

Before we dive into the "how-to" part of listening when a child has a problem, I want to share with you some of my experience as a therapist.

Emotions are okay

A critically important thing to understand about emotions is that they are not "right" or "wrong." They simply exist. Granted, they can be extremely uncomfortable, but that still doesn't make them "wrong." How often have you heard a parent say, "You don't need to be afraid" or "You shouldn't be angry" or "You have no reason to cry"? These comments that are meant to help are actually giving the child the message that being afraid, angry, or unhappy is wrong. When a child receives that message often enough, she begins to feel wrong – defective – as a person. It's more constructive to view uncomfortable emotions as a signal that something needs to change. That's an empowering attitude that helps put those emotions to productive use.

Emotions vs. behavior

Whereas emotions should not be disapproved of or labeled "wrong," behavior resulting from those emotions is a different story. Children need to learn the difference between how they *feel*, and what they *do* with those feelings. When a parent observes the signals her child gives her and then uses supportive understanding to say, "You're so angry at your brother that you feel like punching him!" she's helping her child understand that difference. When you listen to your child and support him in identifying and expressing his emotions, you're teaching him how to deal with his feelings constructively on the behavioral level. He learns that emotions are okay (you have only commented on those emotions, not judged them), whereas infringing on someone else's rights is not okay.

55

Acceptance of emotions

I realize it's sometimes very hard to be accepting of another person's uncomfortable feelings. That's very normal. It's important, though, to keep the idea of acceptance in mind as a goal, because that's the firm base from which a child develops confidence and self-esteem. As a therapist, I have many opportunities to practice this. I often explain to my clients that I can help them best when I have one foot in the pool of problems, "feeling" with them, and the other foot firmly planted on land, where it's clear to me that the problems are not mine (despite the fact that I want to help). That way I can be understanding about how they feel but at the same time I can view their difficulties in an objective manner, from my own vantage point. Even so, this is often a challenge. With one's own child it can be an even greater challenge. There will be times that you just can't keep your child's problem from causing you a problem in some way, as when your child is upset and says something hurtful to you. Then things become more complicated. You find yourself in the red zone, where both of you have problems, and quite possibly you have a conflict with one another. That type of situation will be covered in the last major section of this book.

Emotions have their own "logic"

Here's something I find fascinating about emotions: there are always reasons for them. We don't always discover the reasons, but you can be sure that *if* you had all the pieces of the puzzle, they would fit together. Always assume that there are valid reasons for someone's feelings being what they are. This sounds very idealistic, but isn't it actually true? Consider a child who cries about a seemingly trivial incident. We might find it hard to understand at first, but when we realize that she overheard an argument between her parents, and that she just found out about her friend's parents separating, the crying is a lot easier to understand.

Sharing makes it easier

Some further thoughts for parents when it comes to children's uncomfortable emotions: an important function we provide is that of an "overflow valve." When you are able to endure your child's difficult feelings without being knocked off balance yourself, you are able to share some of the burden. The emotions become less overwhelming to your child. When you can take the further step of talking about those emotions, you help your child deal with them from a viewpoint that's a step removed. Instead of being totally entrenched in the feelings, he can take a step outside those feelings and observe himself. He realizes that he himself comprises more than what he happens to be feeling right at the moment. Feelings have changed before, and they'll change again. It's easier to cope with uncomfortable feelings knowing that they're transient. Your child is then on the road to understanding himself better.

The goals of supportive understanding

You're already familiar with the use of this skill during problem-free times. That means you're well on your way to being able to use it at times that your child is having difficulty. The goal now is to open the door for your child to let you know how she feels. This can be a very delicate operation! We want to communicate genuine interest but not pressure. The messages we want to get across are:

> "I'm noticing that you're bothered by something."
> "You and your feelings are important to me."
> "I have the time and interest to devote to you."
> "I'd like to hear more about ... if you feel like telling me."
> "I have confidence in your ability to work out problems."

Notice that all of these are wonderful I-messages, because they express the parent's thoughts and feelings. They can be stated explicitly, but don't necessarily have to be. You can convey the message that you're taking the time and have the interest in listening without having to say so in words. Just stopping what you were doing and making eye contact go a long way. The important thing is for the message to get across to your child.

Do you remember the idea of "following a little bit ahead"? That's exactly what we'll be doing in this yellow section of the matrix. We're saying to our child, "I see where you are. I'd like to help you get a little bit further." It's an invitation, an offer of help. When this offer is genuine, it comes across in the body language you use, as well as in what you say. The nonverbal messages show in the expression on your face, the way you use your body, and the physical affection you offer.

At each step of the way, when your child feels that you *support* and *understand* him, and – very importantly – *accept him as a person, despite his uncomfortable feelings*, he has an additional piece of solid ground under his feet. He can then risk taking another step. I picture this process as a cog railway, where the wheels engage with the rail at each point along the way, providing support to move ahead without the risk of falling back. Your child is free to move ahead, processing his problem with your support, knowing that you're right there with him. The feedback I receive from kids tells me that they want and need more of this type of support. Feedback from adults tells me that they would like to have had it from their parents when they were children. As one lucky 17-year-old girl wrote, when asked what her parents have done right, "My mother always listened to me and helped when I had problems. My father listened to me and respected my opinions."

Supportive understanding is one of the most valuable gifts we can give our children. We're helping them move from this:

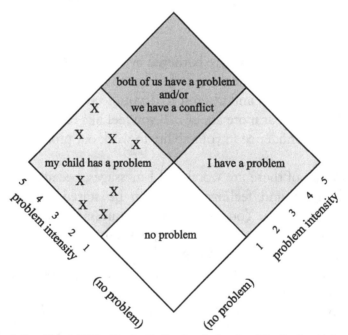

how bothered is my child by this situation?   *how bothered am I by this situation?*

toward this:

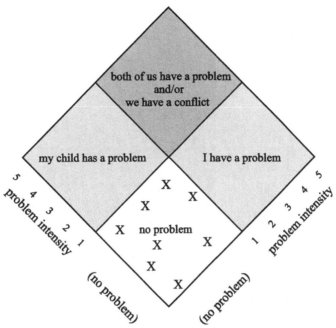

how bothered is my child by this situation?   how bothered am I by this situation?

In the next chapter we'll practice supportive understanding and examine new possibilities this skill offers, now that we've moved from the problem-free zone into the yellow area where your child is dealing with a problem.

7. HOW TO LISTEN SO YOUR CHILD WANTS TO TALK

Before we move on to using supportive understanding, let's make sure we really are in the yellow zone where your child has a problem. How do you know? And how do you know that you don't have a problem? Look back briefly at the lists you made at the beginning of the first chapter, "How I notice that my child is bothered by something" and "How I notice that I am bothered by something." There's a good chance you've become more observant since then, and can add to these lists. If so, go ahead and jot down whatever new points occur to you.

Using (or not using) supportive understanding

Example 1

Here's an interchange between a mother and daughter, before the mother learned about supportive understanding:

> (Daughter comes in from playing outside and looks worried.)
> Mother: Hi! What's wrong?
> Child: Nothing!
> Mother: I'm sure something's bothering you. What's up? You can tell me!
> Child: Nah – nothing, really.
> Mother: Did something happen? You had a problem with someone, didn't you?
> Child: No, that's not it.
> Mother: Just tell me! How can I help if you don't even talk to me?
> Child: Forget it. (goes to bedroom)

It can be a real eye-opener to role play an interchange like this with a friend or partner. How does the "child" feel? Does she feel respected and supported? Does she feel backed into a corner? Given the third degree? Blamed? Does she have the impression that her mother is reaching out to her warmly, or is the mother standing there with her hands on her hips and a demanding look on her face? Are the daughter's needs being met?

Here's the same sequence again, but this time the mother uses supportive understanding several times in a row:

(Daughter comes in from playing outside and looks worried.)
Mother: Hi! (pause) It looks to me as if something's bothering you.
Child: (grunt)
Mother   I'd be interested in hearing, if you feel like telling me anything.
Child: Don't know …
Mother: So you're not sure if you want to talk about it.
Child: Yeah.
Mother: Aha …
Child: Yeah, I'm afraid you'll get mad at me.
Mother: So you're uneasy about how I might react.
Child: Right! Will you promise not to yell at me?
Mother: Okay – I'll do my best not to get angry.
Child: Well … this is what happened (and proceeds to tell how another girl grabbed her jacket while they were playing, and now it's ripped).

Now let's analyze exactly what happened in the second version, a real-life example, using symbols and comments. We'll be using the same symbols as we did before: a *video camera* for a factual description of the situation, a *heart* for the feelings, and *arrows* for practical results.

(Daughter comes in from playing outside and looks worried.) ♥

Mother: Hi! (pause) It looks to me as if something's bothering you. ♥

This is a counterpart to "You look happy," for example, in the problem-free

area. The mother is commenting on the child's emotional state.

Child: (grunt)

The child is not ready to communicate much.

Mother: I'd be interested ♥ in hearing, if you feel like ♥ telling me

anything.

The mother doesn't push. Instead, she indicates her readiness to listen, and leaves the decision about "telling anything" to the child.

Child: Don't know … ♥

The child voices uncertainty.

Mother: So you're not sure ♥ if you want to talk about it.

The mother is mirroring back – in her own words – the child's feelings.

Child: Yeah.

The child verifies that the mother is absolutely on track. She doesn't offer any new information, though.

Mother: Aha …

The mother stays right there where the child is, emotionally; she is respectful, doesn't push, and doesn't go too fast.

Child: Yeah, I'm afraid ♥ you'll get mad ♥ at me.

The child seems reassured that the mother really understands. (The cogs are engaged!) Now she's prepared to take the step of revealing more.

Mother: So you're uneasy ♥ about how I might react.

The mother now mirrors this new information

Child: Right! Will you promise not to yell at me?

The child again verifies that the mother has understood, and is ready to talk if she's sure she won't be chastised.

Mother: Okay – I'll do my best not to get angry. ♥

Child: Well … this is what happened … (and proceeds to tell how another girl grabbed her jacket while they were playing, ✖ and now it's ripped). ⚡

What's really enlightening about this interchange is the abundance of hearts: the most important steps took place on the emotional level. The discussion had a lot to do with interest and respect (on the mother's part) and trust (on the daughter's part). It wasn't until all of this was cleared up that anything factual came up for discussion. Before that, the mother had no idea what had happened. All she could work with was the emotional level. The common emotional ground she built with her daughter was the necessary foundation for going any further.

Example 2

Here's another example where the father hasn't yet learned about supportive understanding:

> (Son comes home from school and is obviously angry.)
> Child: I'm not going to school any more!
> Father: What kind of attitude is that?
> Child: I hate my teacher!
> Father: Well, you can't like everyone in life.
> Child: I'm just not going!
> Father: Of course you are! How can you get a good job later if you don't go to school?
> Child: (mutters something and disappears)

Again, try role playing this short sequence with someone. What sorts of feelings is the "child" left with afterwards? Does he feel understood and taken seriously? Does he feel his father is preaching to him? That he's being ordered around?

Let's have a look at the same situation, but now the father knows about supportive understanding:

> (Son comes home from school and is obviously angry.)
> Child: I'm not going to school any more!
> Father: You're really bothered about something!
> Child: Yeah, and I hate my teacher most of all.
> Father: And you're especially annoyed at him.

Child: Yeah, he's really unfair.
Father: So something he did feels unjust to you.
Child: Right. We didn't have any gym today.
Father: Oh – you expected to have gym but then you didn't.
Child: Just because some of the other kids were bad.
Father: So all of you got punished for something a few kids did.
Child: Yeah! That's really unfair!
Father: You were really disappointed not to have gym today.
Child: Yeah. I think I'll talk to him about that tomorrow. He shouldn't punish all of us when only a few kids did something wrong! (He then trots off and seems perfectly okay.)

Now here's a closer look at what happened in this discussion, another real-life sequence:

(Son comes home from school and is obviously angry.) ♥

Child: I'm not going to school any more! ✖

The child makes his feelings known and announces his plans.

Father: You're really bothered ♥ about something!

The father mirrors the child's emotional state.

Child: Yeah, and I hate my teacher most of all. ♥

The child verifies that the father is on the right track, then gives more information.

Father: And you're especially annoyed at him. ♥

The father again mirrors the child's feelings, more specifically now.

Child: Yeah, he's really unfair. ♥

The child gives additional information.

Father: So something he did ✖ feels unjust to you. ♥

More mirroring, helping the child to be more specific, but without prying.

65

Child: Right. We didn't have any gym today. ✗

The child comes out with part of what's bothering him.

Father: Oh – you expected to have gym but then you didn't. ✗

The father mirrors the new information to be sure he's understanding correctly. His tone of voice lets his son know that he can imagine how the child feels about that.

Child: Just because some of the other kids were bad. ✗

More details from the child.

Father: So all of you got punished for something a few kids did. ✗

Father summarizes what he's understood so far, and – nonverbally – lets his child feel his supportive stance.

Child: Yeah! That's really unfair! ♥

The child has gone from having a generalized feeling of anger to expressing specifically what's bothering him: being treated unfairly.

Father: You were really disappointed ♥ not to have gym today. ✗

The father is homing in on another strong emotion: disappointment.

Child: Yeah. I think I'll talk to him about that tomorrow. ✗
            He shouldn't punish all of us when only a few kids did
            something wrong! (He then trots off and seems perfectly
            okay.) ♥

The child no longer feels any need to deal with his feelings. He's now moved on to planning a practical solution to the problem, and is satisfied (and has changed his mind about going to school!).

What have we witnessed this time? There was a lot of emotional work in this example, too. At each step (when the "cogs" engaged) the child felt understood and supported. He then offered more details, and the father helped him reach the next step.

It was gratifying to watch how the vague emotion of anger became more concrete. It became clear to the child that he was feeling unjustly treated, and that he was disappointed (probably not only about missing gym, but also about the teacher's actions).

Did you notice that the child came up with his own solution, without the least bit of practical help from anyone else? This happens often, once the emotions have been recognized, acknowledged, and supported by the parent. It's a wonderful phenomenon. Why? We're helping our kids grow toward independence and responsibility. This is how children build confidence in their own capabilities to deal with their own challenges!

Where to be especially careful

Less is more

One of the biggest challenges in implementing supportive understanding is holding yourself back when you want to ask questions or give suggestions. It's only natural for a parent to want more information, and faster. It's also very natural to want to offer suggestions when your child is having difficulty. After all, we have much more life experience behind us than our children do. We're often several steps ahead. That can result in what I like to call the "*yes, but*" syndrome: "*yes*, I hear you, *but* you should look at it this way," or "*yes*, I hear you, *but* you shouldn't feel that way." Our aim with supportive understanding is to concentrate on the "*yes*" and make it really important: "*yes*, I understand what you mean" and "*yes*, I can imagine how you feel." Bite your tongue when you feel the urge to utter the "*but*" because that word goes a long way toward negating the "*yes*" part of what you say. Just imagine your partner telling you, "I love you, but ..."!

You will see that in these situations, "less is more," as the saying goes. In the first rendition of our first example, all the mother's questions got her nowhere. (As one 17-year-old girl wrote, her biggest gripe about her mother was "*always* questioning me about *everything*.") Her daughter didn't get very far, either. In the first version of the second example, all the good information being offered by the father only served to have his son withdraw from the scene.

I know how hard it can be to stick with only what your child is offering at each step. It will be worth it, though, once you get the hang of things. It's helpful to make believe you're a reporter, commenting on what you observe. In this case you're commenting, most importantly, on the emotions you're noticing ("You were really disappointed ..."), and you're commenting on the factual information your child gives ("... not to have gym today"). *Don't ask any questions,* and *don't offer any additional information or suggestions* at this stage! Granted, this is arbitrary, but it's the best way to master the capability of supportive understanding. Later on – *much* later on – you can be more lax about how you implement this form of communication. Right now, stick to the rules for the best results. It's like learning a new sport and deciding to stick to the advice you get from the pro, then developing your own style later, when you're more skilled in the basics.

Why no questions?

You may be wondering what's wrong with asking questions or offering additional information. Doing so often leads the child down a path that he wouldn't have chosen himself, or that isn't the most productive way for him to make progress. It artificially narrows the field of possibilities. One question that we parents are especially fond of asking is "why?". "Why did you do that?" or "Why are you so unhappy?" It seems, though, that "why" often makes the child feel backed up against a wall. It can come across as an accusation, or a demand to justify his emotions. Even adults often don't know why they feel what they feel. For children it's even more of a challenge.

Here and now

You can help your child put problems into a more manageable perspective by emphasizing the temporary nature of the situation, the "here and now." When your child's friends happen to be busy and she says, "There's *never* anyone to play with!" you can comment, "Right now you don't have a playmate." This response reminds her gently that this is a momentary problem, not a chronic one. As I mentioned in the last chapter, you're being her "overflow valve," helping her to manage her emotions without being overwhelmed. She remembers that this has happened before, that she managed to get through the problem then, and that she'll be able to do so again this time.

Staying on target

A very good way of making sure you stay on track is to preface every comment you make with the phrase, "just so I understand you, ..." or another one with the same meaning. You don't even need to say it out loud, but you should think it to yourself every single time. That phrase works magic! Doing it that way minimizes the chances of lapsing into questions or suggestions before you realize what you're doing.

When you mess up

And when you realize what you're doing, but the words are already out of your mouth – what then? Pat yourself on the back, because you've made an important first step. Noticing what you could have done better means you're making real progress! Some parents become discouraged at this stage, because they begin to realize what they could have been doing better all along. If that happens to you, try to use the realization in a positive way. We all have room for improvement, no matter where we happen to be in the process. Your child will sense that you're trying your best.

Anger: a special emotion

"Getting mad" is a curious phenomenon. Who doesn't know what it feels like to be angry? It's one of the basic human emotions, along with feelings like sadness, fear, excitement, and so forth. In my experience, though, the state of anger often serves to cover up other emotions. Think back to the example of the boy whose teacher cancelled gym class. What he was really feeling was resentment at being treated unjustly, and disappointment over the change in plans. It started out as diffuse anger, though, and through the processing with his father he became aware of his deeper feelings. When I'm driving on the highway and some aggressive driver cuts me off, I get angry. I soon realize, though, that I feel some deeper emotions. Momentarily I feared for my safety, I feel disrespectfully treated, and I am frustrated at having been the potential victim of an unsafe driver. Try looking back at some of the times you've been angry or annoyed at someone (even yourself). If you scratch away at the feelings on the surface, you just may discover some other emotions beneath.

Somehow, anger (and annoyance, a milder form) are easier for many people to feel and recognize. It takes some digging to discover what feelings lie beneath. Sometimes those other feelings are more uncomfortable, making people feel weak or vulnerable, or are less socially acceptable. When you're using supportive understanding with your child, keep your eyes and ears open for other feelings that may be underneath an initial outburst of anger.

Examples for practice

Here's a partial list of "uncomfortable" emotions, just so you aren't at a loss for ideas! They're arranged in groups of overlapping terms.

> abandoned, afraid, anxious, cautious, concerned, frightened, hesitant, nervous
> angry, defiant, furious, hateful, jealous, resentful, spiteful, stubborn, vengeful
> confused, distrustful, doubtful, hesitant, insecure, uncertain
> abandoned, disappointed, heartbroken, helpless, hurt, offended, shocked
> annoyed, frustrated, grumpy, impatient, irritated, upset
> depressed, grieving, helpless, hopeless, lonely, moody, regretful, sad
> disgraced, embarrassed, humiliated, remorseful, shamed, weak

For purposes of the following exercises, let's assume that you yourself are in the problem-free area. Now you notice that your child is bothered by something. Try your hand at forming some good comments that show support and understanding.

1. There's been a disagreement, and now your 10-year-old screams, "I hate you!"

   ....

2. Your four-year-old skins her knee and starts crying.

   ....

3. Your daughter of fourteen arrives home looking as if she just saw a ghost.

   ....

4. Your son of twelve looks nervous and says he's "not home" if a certain friend comes to the door.

   ....

5. Your seven-year-old is trying to do homework but throws his notebook on the floor in frustration.

   ....

6. Your three-year-old has a tantrum because you won't buy something he wants.

   ....

There's no telling how these hypothetical conversations would develop, but here are some of my ideas as to how a parent could start out with supportive understanding:

1. "Wow, you're really angry at me!" ♥

2. "Oh, dear! That scraped knee ♣ must hurt a lot." ♥

3. "You look very frightened!" ♥

4. "It sounds as if you don't want anything to do with him ♥ right now." ♣

5. "It looks as if you're having difficulty ♥ with your homework." ♣

6. "I know you'd really, really like ♥ me to buy that ♣ for you!"

As you see, at the outset we sometimes don't know much about the circumstances leading to the emotions. Just start with whatever you notice – *no more and no less* – and take it from there.

Individual and situational factors

There are certain basic requirements that need to be fulfilled in order for supportive understanding to function well. I like to group them into three categories: *parent*, *child*, and *situation*. Here are some points to consider:

important for the parent:
> Are you interested right now?
> Do you have time right now?
> Are you in the no-problem zone yourself?
> – or –
> Can you at least put your own difficulties aside for now?

important for the child:
> Is he interested in talking about the problem right now?
> Does he trust the parent enough to confide in her?

important about the situation:
> Is the setting appropriate?

Practicing on your own

You can continue practicing this type of communication whenever you notice that your child is troubled by something. There's a chart at this end of the chapter for recording some of your experiences using supportive understanding. This one-page chart is intended to be used for one "session," which will often involve several interchanges between you and your child. As with the charts in previous chapters, it's worth having some copies handy.

Practical problem-solving
You'll find that when the emotional level of a problem has been dealt with satisfactorily, there often comes a point where your child is ready to attack

the problem on a practical level. There are many useful ways of providing help if your child wants support; you'll find information on that topic in Appendix 1.

More than one child

You may be wondering what to do when more than one child is involved. The goal then is to give supportive understanding to each child. Besides providing that support for each child, you function as a type of interpreter, helping each child understand the other, as you mirror each one's feelings. It's exactly what you've been doing with one child, only now you're dealing with two (or more) in parallel. Just remember to give each one sufficient time and attention.

Very young children

What if your child is too young to understand words? Then the nonverbal level becomes the main vehicle of communication. This includes tone of voice, gestures, facial expression, physical contact, and so forth. The whole category of nonverbal expression is extremely important anyhow, even with older children, because actions really do speak louder than words. The verbal communication serves as a more precise way of clarifying the situation, to whatever extent your child is capable of doing so. Think about comforting an infant who's teething. You might be saying, "Oh, my little fellow – that must really hurt!" as you're soothing and comforting him, but you could just as well be telling him the days of the week. It's the nonverbal elements that convey the message.

It takes time, but ...

Are you wondering how time-consuming this method of communication will be? Yes, supportive understanding does take more time than communicating in the more traditional ways – but only short-term. In the long run, you're making a great investment in your child's ability to take care of her own problems, with less and less support needed from you as time goes on. You're teaching your child to take responsibility for herself and her own well-being. Besides that, you're making a wonderful investment in the relationship.

Sometimes the time isn't right

If you want to help your child, but the situation isn't appropriate just now, for instance, you can say, "I'd be glad to talk about that. What about after lunch when we're alone?" That way your child knows that you're interested and will get back to her.

Sometimes your child won't feel like being "understood." Have you ever needed to clear something up in your own mind first, before confiding in someone else? That's normal, and people vary on that score. Some people work through their problems best when talking about them, and other people need more solitude. If you think that's happening with your child, you can voice your observation with a comment like, "I guess you don't feel like talking now. But I'm here if you need me."

Emergencies

Of course there are very urgent situations when you need to act immediately, as in a medical emergency, and there's no time to offer support and understanding. Those are real exceptions, though. In most situations there's room for supportive understanding when your child is experiencing a problem. For instance, if your child needs to have a wound stitched and she refuses to cooperate, that's an opportunity to show her that you understand she's afraid. Then you can give her some small measure of influence over the situation by finding out what could make the ordeal less dramatic for her.

Other ways to practice

In additional to practicing with your child, it's good to practice supportive understanding by role playing with a friend who's interested in learning this skill. Here's a good way to show you how well the "person with the problem" feels understood: take a rope and start out with one of you close to each end. After each supportive statement, the person with the problem decides how well understood she feels, then moves appropriately along the rope – toward or away from the supporting person. This gives clear feedback as to how the exercise is going. Another way to do it is to start out on opposite sides of the room, and adjust the distance from there.

Try and try again

The skill you're learning is a special gift that needs attention over the course of a lifetime. Try to remember that the goal is not perfection, but rather to do the best you can. All your efforts will be richly rewarded! My course participants tell me that they often recognize only afterwards that they could have done better in certain situations. That's not failure; it's progress! In the courses, we take some of these situations and analyze what happened and what can be done differently the next time. You have this chance, too. There's guaranteed to be a "next time" in your family.

Just so you know that I, too, catch myself doing things less than ideally, let me tell you about something that happened just recently with my youngest son, who's eleven. He was complaining about the lunches at school. I was proud of the way I conversed with him. (I was in a good frame of mind and had enough time right then!) He ended up feeling much better and came up with a plan for the next time the food was so "disgusting." Then he said to me, "Mommy, I really like talking to you about things!" I felt good. The story goes on, however. On that particular day, he was eager to get out and play in the snow, but knew he should do his homework first. Lo and behold, the paper he needed in order to do his assignment was nowhere to be found. The next morning, as he was packing a snack into his schoolbag, the missing paper appeared miraculously. I said, with exasperation, "If you had looked for it a little bit more thoroughly yesterday, you would have found it and been able to do your homework." I knew I was right. He glared at me and replied, "You know what? I hate talking to people who think they know everything all the time!" We all mess it up sometimes. Just try again the next time.

The matrix

At the end of the previous section on the problem-free area, we took a look at the matrix from the viewpoint of our responsibilities as parents. As we come to the end of this section, we can fill in the portion of the matrix that we've dealt with here. In the zone where our child has a problem, our responsibility is to offer him the support and understanding he needs to be able to move ahead with problem-solving on his own.

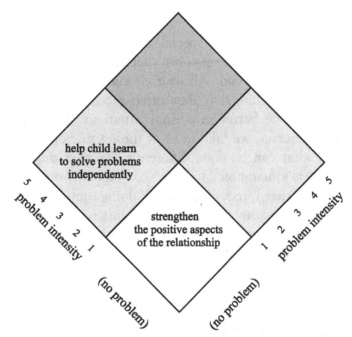

how bothered is my child by this situation?   how bothered am I by this situation?

In the next section we'll see what to do in the yellow zone where you are having a problem.

Work Sheet: **Supportive Understanding when my child has a problem**

date:

	situation:	result (feelings):	result (practical):

what I said:

child's reaction:

what I said:

child's reaction:

what I said:

child's reaction:

what I said:

child's reaction:

…

…

…

…

results, changes, etc.:

I have a problem

HOW TO HELP YOURSELF WITH PROBLEMS

---

8. WHY TALK TO YOUR CHILD IF YOU HAVE A PROBLEM?

Parental goals

Let's look yet again at the parenting goal I proposed earlier, with regard to my own children: "I hope they will be able to fulfill their own needs and desires and, at the same time, respect other people's right to do the same." In the previous section we talked about helping our children to fulfill the first part of this goal. Our children can learn to fulfill the second part of the goal

79

by becoming sensitive to *other* people and *their* needs and desires, at the same time as they are learning to fulfill their own needs and desires. A different way of saying this is: children can learn to notice and respect the boundaries where other people's rights begin. This is another wonderful opportunity for growth – for our children, for our relationships with our children, and for ourselves. In this section we'll see why it's important to make our own personal thresholds known to our children, and how we can do that in a constructive manner.

What do children need in order to become more sensitive to our needs, desires, and feelings when we ourselves have a problem? They need clear information without blame or judgement. "I'm not feeling so great right now, and would really appreciate some quiet" is a clear message. It's much more informative than "You're being too loud!" It's also better, because the child is getting a message that doesn't make her feel backed into a corner. There's no blame. The I-messages that we learned about in Chapter 5 are an ideal way of communicating when we have a problem.

Using I-messages

Since you're already familiar with the use of this skill during problem-free times, you have the basic preparation for applying it at times when you find yourself having a problem. The goal here, in this yellow zone, is to give your child information about you and your problem, and to do it in such a way that your child *wants to listen* to you. The messages we try to get across are:

> "I'm noticing that I'm bothered by something."
> "It's important to me to communicate my feelings to you."
> "I hope you're interested."
> "I'd like your help in solving my problem."

As with supportive understanding, it's not necessary to say these things in so many words. What's important is getting the ideas across to your child.

In this section, your main goal is to move from this:

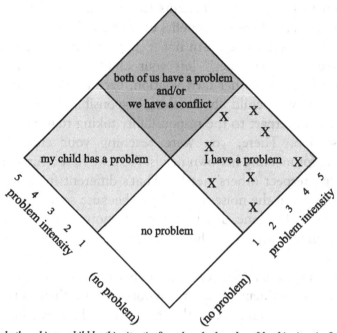

how bothered is my child by this situation?   *how bothered am I by this situation?*

toward this:

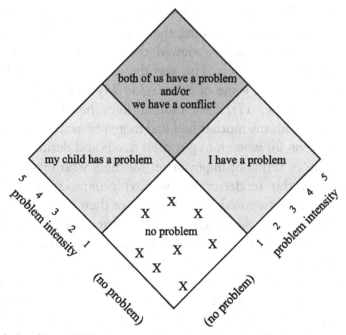

how bothered is my child by this situation?   *how bothered am I by this situation?*

Giving your child a choice

In addition to the potential benefits to yourself of communicating when you have a problem, there are benefits to your child. A good I-message gives your child the choice to act. "I'm not feeling so great right now and would really appreciate some quiet!" lets your child decide to turn down the volume, and to do so of her own volition, because she wants to help you. You're teaching your child about taking responsibility for her own actions. (This is the counterpart to the responsibility taking that we talked about in the last section. There, you were teaching your child how to take responsibility for meeting her own needs. Here we're teaching children about how they can respect others' needs.) That's different from following orders (for instance, "Turn the noise down!") just because someone, even a parent, demands that it be done. It's important to note that although the same action (turning down the volume) comes about, the process is a very different one.

From a developmental viewpoint, it's important for children to experience the capability of influencing their environment by their actions. Children learn that their behavior affects other people and their reactions.

Being a role model

When you use I-messages you're setting a good example for your child. You're being a role model, showing that you take care of yourself. Many of the participants in my survey viewed their parents (and especially their mothers) as poor role models. This was the case for both the teenagers and the adults. Here's what some of them said: "My mother should take better care of herself" (boy, 17); "My mother lives her life for other people" (woman, 43); "I wish my mother had had more self-respect" (woman, 47).

It's very common for women to put their needs and desires at the bottom of the totem pole in terms of importance. Mothers who model good self-care help counteract this tendency in the next generation. Children learn by example. Girls see how to take healthy care of their needs, and boys see that it's good for females to do so. One course participant told me recently that she was thrilled to have ways of talking to her children about problems without having to sacrifice her own individuality.

It's important to set a good example in this area, because it will be valuable for your child in future relationships. Think about the difference between "I'm frustrated that I had to wait here so long for you" and "You're really undependable." In the first case the parent is stating her own feelings and the circumstances that led to those feelings. She's giving potentially useful information to her child. In the second case, the parent is simply name-calling. There isn't anything constructive that can come out of that for either the parent or the child. Your own particular ways of dealing with difficulties will most likely rub off on your child.

Talking about emotions

I-messages teach children that, within a trusting relationship, it's good to talk about feelings, and that something beneficial often comes out of such discussions. This is just as true here, where the parent has a problem, as it is in situations where the child has a problem. Many people shy away from discussing emotions, especially when the emotions are unpleasant. Yet those are the times when it's especially important to be able to do exactly that! In this way, we learn more about ourselves and about the other person, and that goes for parents as well as children. The more we understand what's going on within ourselves and within the other person, the easier it is to solve problems.

Our children usually want to know more about us and how we're feeling. Here are more comments from the survey: "My mother doesn't talk openly enough with me about her problems" (girl, 17); "My father is too closed. I don't know what's wrong or how I can help him" (boy, 17); "My father should express his thoughts and feelings more" (girl, 17); "I wish my father had shown his emotions" (woman, 36).

Improving relationships

That leads to the next benefit: the relationship gets better. The more time we spend in the problem-free zone with someone, the more energy we have for the enjoyable aspects of the relationship. And the better we understand one another, the deeper the relationship can become. I-messages ask the implicit question, "Are you interested in hearing something about me, what I think, how I feel?" That's the flip side of the message we're giving when we use supportive understanding: "I'd like to hear more about ... if you feel like telling me."

Developing a conscience

When we communicate our values clearly to our children, we're helping them develop and hone their feelings of conscience. A small child who hits the family pet learns after a while not to do that because the parents disapprove of such actions. Slowly but surely the child internalizes the idea that it's "not right" to hurt pets. This is now the child's own conviction, not just the parents' belief. The child then doesn't hit the pet even when there's no parent around to witness the act, because the child's own conscience comes into play.

Realizing when they're not responsible

Parents often wonder whether they should even mention anything to their children when they're having problems themselves. Shouldn't adults just take care of their own difficulties? It's not as simple as that. Children often feel responsible for causing unfortunate events even when that's not actually the case, as when their parents have separated. I-messages can help set things straight. Clear information ("I'm short on patience right now because Mommy and Daddy are having trouble getting along with each other.") provides relief to a child who wonders what he's done wrong to "cause" his parent to be impatient. It's like finding out that your grumpy spouse had a hard time at work and that the moodiness really has nothing to do with you. It's a relief to have that information.

Getting cooperation

There's something else to be said for using I-messages. They have the beneficial side effect of maximizing the chances that your child wants to cooperate. Consider how you'd feel, on the other hand, if someone who's important to you said, "You're really undependable!" What might your reaction be? Would you be highly motivated to help out the person who said that to you? You'd probably be too busy resenting the comment or defending yourself. And if that person said to you, instead, "I'm frustrated that I had to wait here so long for you," how would you feel? Even if you didn't want to hear that, you might have a bit more desire to put yourself in the other person's shoes. We're generally more motivated to help someone who states his own problem – which is an implicit request for help – rather than criticizing us. We feel less need to be on the defensive.

Here's a great story I heard toward the end of one of my recent courses. Prior to the course, one particular family had been having real battles over sharing the household chores. It was especially difficult for the mother to get her thirteen-year-old son to cooperate and contribute. One day, however, she reported that she'd almost keeled over when she happened to overhear her son saying to his younger sister, "Listen, you can help, too! You know how much work Mom has around here!"

Person vs. behavior

Do you remember the idea of accepting your child as a person, despite his uncomfortable feelings when he has a problem? That was a major goal in the use of supportive understanding. When using I-messages, there's an important goal that is similar. When you're having a problem because of something your child has done, try to restrict your disapproval to the child's behavior, rather than the child as a person. "You're really undependable" is a criticism of the entire person. "We agreed to meet half an hour ago but you weren't here" is an objection to the child's behavior (and that's why "I'm frustrated that I had to wait here so long for you"). A child needs to feel *accepted as a person, despite the fact that you disapprove of her behavior*. This, of course, is easier said than done. (In fact, some people wonder whether it's even possible to distinguish between a person and what that person does.) My own conviction is that we should make that distinction as clearly as we can. I view this as another one of those goals that we parents can set for ourselves, knowing we'll never be perfect. We do the best we can under whatever the circumstances happen to be.

Punishment and consequences

Oh, is this a controversial topic! Why not just punish a child for his "bad" behavior, instead of going into long-winded explanations? In my opinion, punishment is harmful to the relationship between child and parent. How would you feel if your partner punished you when you did something that wasn't to his liking? (Maybe you've even experienced this firsthand.) How did you feel as a child when you got punished? Try to think back to some specific occasions. Were you eager to please your parents and do better the next time? Or did you feel resentful and want to "get back" at them for punishing you? Maybe you felt like lying to them. Perhaps you began keeping your feelings to yourself. Why would your child feel any differently?

Punishment also tends to distract from the significant issues at hand. We've been practicing the skills needed to focus on the child's behavior, and how that behavior overstepped the other person's boundaries (or infringed on the other person's rights). Punishment tends to come across to the child as something arbitrary dished out by the parent. Then the child is often so involved in his own reaction to the punishment that it's difficult for him to see things from the parent's viewpoint. That's counterproductive, and is one big reason that punishment basically doesn't work, long-term.

Many parents are of the opinion that "I was punished as a kid, and I didn't turn out any worse for it" or "If it didn't hurt me, it won't hurt my kid." I've worked with many such parents. What usually happens over the course of time is that they realize how humiliated and hurt they really did feel sometimes as children. They don't want to do the same thing to their own kids. It's often difficult when we realize that our parents weren't perfect and that we resent some of the things they did.

What about "consequences"? There's a lot of talk about "natural" and "logical" consequences as opposed to "artificial" consequences. An example of a natural consequence is feeling cold outside because of wearing insufficient clothing. An artificial consequence would be grounding a teenager who got home too late from a date. That type of consequence is viewed by some parents, though, as acceptable and "natural" because it is related to the "crime" of missing the curfew, making it seem "logical" to the parents. It's helpful for parents to ask themselves whether the consequence occurred on its own (as a natural result of something else) – a natural consequence – or whether it occurred because the parent decided it should happen – an artificial consequence. Even if the artificial consequence is related to what the child did, and therefore seems logical, it will be felt by the child to be a punishment imposed on him by the parent.

It's important to look inside ourselves and ask what our reasons are for punishing. Often it's a last resort when nothing else seems to work and we feel as though we've run out of options. We'll talk more about this in the next chapter, where we'll practice much more effective ways of addressing children's behavior when it causes us problems.

9. HOW TO TALK SO YOUR CHILD WANTS TO LISTEN

Before going on to practice I-messages, let's check that we really are in the yellow zone where you have a problem. How do you know? And how do you know that your child doesn't have one? As I suggested when we began practicing in the other yellow zone a couple of chapters back, have another look at the lists you made in the first chapter, "How I notice that my child is bothered by something" and "How I notice that I am bothered by something." You may be able to add more to these lists, based on observations you've made in the meantime.

Using (or not using) I-messages

Example 1

Here's an exchange between a mother and son, before the mother knew about I-messages:

> (Son comes in from playing outside, happy as can be and covered with mud.)
> Mother: Look what a slob you are!
> Child: (looking surprised) I am not! I was just playing.
> Mother: Of course you are. Look at all that mud on your pants.
> Child: But I couldn't help it!
> Mother: Yeah, sure. Why can't you be more careful? That's really inconsiderate of you.
> Child: But it wasn't my fault! A kid pushed me and I fell.
> Mother: I'm not interested in hearing excuses. No more playing outside this week!
> Child: (crying) I hate you! You're so mean!

What's really been accomplished here? Try role playing this sequence with a friend or partner. How does the "child" feel? Does he still feel as though his mother likes and approves of him as a person, despite the mud? Is it clear to him why his mother is so annoyed? Does he feel that he is being devalued as a person? Does he feel backed into a corner, having to defend himself? How does the "mother" feel? Does she think her son understands her reasons for being irritated? Does she feel good about herself and how she handled the situation? Is she frustrated? Does she wonder how things between them could deteriorate so quickly? Notice that the child, who started out in the problem-free area, now has a problem. The mother still has a problem. The situation has escalated into a conflict between the two of them; they are in the red zone. Nobody is happy. Nobody's needs or desires are being met.

Here's the same situation again, but this time the mother uses I-messages:

> (Son comes in from playing outside, happy as can be and covered with mud.)
> Mother: Oh, no! Look at all that mud! I wasn't expecting you to look like that!
> Child: (looking surprised) Oh, yeah. I guess my pants are really dirty.
> Mother: Hm ... that's a problem for me. Those pants are so dirty that I can't even put them in the washing machine like that! And I just don't feel like washing them by hand right now.
> Child: That's okay, Mom. I'll do it for you!
> Mother: I like that idea!

Most of you are probably thinking, "Yeah, sure!" My class participants say the same thing – and then come back the next week reporting similar experiences! Let's have a close look at just what happened in this second version, another real-life example, using symbols and comments. We'll be using the same symbols as we did before: a *video camera* for a factual description of the situation, a *heart* for the feelings, and *arrows* for practical results.

(Son comes in from playing outside, happy as can be ♥ and covered with mud.) 📹

The child has no apparent problem.

Mother: Oh, no! Look at all that mud! 📹 I wasn't expecting you to look like that! ♥

The mother is describing what she sees, and her feeling of being unpleasantly surprised. Her son has done something that's a problem for her.

Child: (looking surprised) ♥ Oh, yeah. I guess my pants are really dirty. ✗

The child is still in the problem-free area.

Mother: Hm ... that's a problem for me. ♥ Those pants are so dirty ✗ that I can't even put them in the washing machine like that! ✗ And I just don't feel like washing them by hand right now. ♥

The mother now states explicitly that she has a problem with the muddy pants. She explains the practical results, and more about her feelings.

Child: That's okay, Mom. ♥ I'll do it for you! ✗

The child is motivated to help his mother solve the problem and offers a practical solution.

Mother: I like that idea! ♥

The mother is back in the problem-free area.

In this interchange, the mother's approach enabled her child to stay in the problem-free zone, even though she herself was in the zone where she had a problem. Since the child was not labeled by his mother as being "a bad child," he felt no need to be defensive. Instead, he was able to concentrate on helping to solve the problem. The mother was nevertheless able to let the child know clearly that she wasn't happy about the muddy pants. The situation did not escalate, and there were no hard feelings. The mother and son quickly found themselves back in the problem-free area together. Notice that both treated each other with respect the entire time.

This is a good time to talk a bit more about "consequences." In the first version of this example, the mother decided on the "consequence" that her son wouldn't be allowed to play outside any more that week. That would solve the mud dilemma, wouldn't it? The "consequence" was something that the mother selected arbitrarily. That's another way of saying "punishment." According to Webster's Unabridged Dictionary, a punishment is "a penalty inflicted for an offense, fault, etc." The key word, for our purposes, is "inflicted." A punishment is a penalty (or consequence) that's decided upon by someone: an artificial consequence. In the second version of our example, the mother explained the natural consequence that the muddy pants would have to be hand washed before they could be put into the washing machine. That had a very different feeling to it from the punishment! It was a direct result of the circumstances, not an arbitrary decision, and was therefore much easier for the child to understand and accept.

Example 2

Here's another example where the mother hasn't yet learned about I-messages (or maybe she does know about them but isn't able to get it all together right at the moment):

> (Mother is getting ready to go out and discovers her makeup supply has been raided.)
> Mother: That was pretty sneaky of you, taking my makeup without permission!
> Teen: (silence)
> Mother: Who do you think you are, just taking my stuff?
> Teen: (rolls eyes heavenward)
> Mother: Answer me! Where do you get the nerve? You have your own makeup.
> Teen: Oh, just leave me alone!

Try out the roles of mother and daughter in this non-conversation. What does the daughter think and feel? What about the mother? You probably already have a good idea about how to do things differently.

Let's look at the same situation, but with the use of I-messages on the mother's part:

(Mother is getting ready to go out and discovers her makeup supply has been raided.)

Mother: (unpleasantly surprised) Hey, half my makeup is missing!

Teen: (silence)

Mother: I have to leave soon, and now I don't have what I need. This is really frustrating!

Teen: (sheepishly) Yeah, I felt like experimenting last night when you were out.

Mother: I'd really appreciate it if you'd ask me first, instead of just taking stuff.

Teen: Yeah, you're right. Sorry. It's all in my room – I'll just go get it for you.

Once again, let's take a closer look at what happened in this short discussion:

(Mother is getting ready to go out and discovers her makeup supply has been raided.)

Mother: (unpleasantly surprised) Hey, half my makeup is missing! ♥ ♟

The mother is stating a fact, and her tone makes it clear that she's not happy.

Teen: (silence)

Mother: I have to leave soon, ♟ and now I don't have what I need. ✗ This is really frustrating! ♥

The mother is giving more information about her dilemma and her feelings.

Teen: (sheepishly) ♥ Yeah, I felt like experimenting ♥ last night when you were out. ♟

The daughter feels badly and defends herself, explaining her reason.

Mother: I'd really appreciate it ♥ if you'd ask me first, instead of just taking stuff. ♟

The mother offers an alternative that would have been acceptable to her.

Teen: Yeah, you're right. Sorry. ♥ It's all in my room – I'll just go get it for you.

The daughter understands the mother's viewpoint and does what she can to remedy the situation.

What happened this time? The mother refrained from making accusations about the daughter's character, sticking instead to the facts. She stated clearly what bothered her and how she felt. The daughter moved very briefly into the area where she, too, had a problem (she felt guilty about what she'd done) but was able to move back into a problem-free state quickly. She could do so because her mother continued on a constructive path, using I-messages. Then the daughter was both willing and able to work with her mother, not against her.

In both versions of this last example, we began with a situation in which the parent had a problem and the child didn't. In the process of confronting the child with her actions, the situation became problematic for the child, too (although much less so in the second version than in the first). This happens often. After all, who likes to be told that something she did was a problem for someone else? In terms of our matrix, we then find ourselves in the red zone, where there's a conflict. We'll go into that area more deeply in the next section of this book. What's especially noteworthy here is how well I-messages work to minimize conflicts and escalation of hard feelings.

Where to be especially careful

"You-messages"
There's something very subtle about a genuine I-message. It has to be a reflection of what the parent is feeling, and not a hidden criticism of the child. Sometimes it's difficult to detect the difference. Examples of "you-messages" that look like I-messages at first glance are: "I feel as if you're really inconsiderate" or "I have a problem with you being so unreliable." In the first instance, a real I-message might be "I was hoping you'd clean up after yourself in the bathroom – I'm a little disappointed" or, in the second

case, "I was depending on you being home at a certain time, and I'm frustrated because now we'll be late for the appointment." It helps to think about the elements that we've been identifying with symbols: the situation at hand, the feelings, and the practical results. A "you-message" tends not to contain these important elements. Instead, it criticizes the child, probably making him feel defective, rather than stating that the parent is having a problem.

Even with the most well-formulated I messages, it sometimes happens that a child takes offense. Perhaps the child isn't interested in hearing how you feel right then. Maybe your I-message has resulted in the child having a problem, too, in which case you're in the red area together. As you know, you still have that part of the book ahead of you!

Here and now

As with supportive understanding, it's useful to concentrate on the current situation. Instead of saying, "You *always* leave your shoes in the hallway and they're in my way," you can say, "Your shoes are in the hallway and they're in my way." That's more concrete and offers the child a chance to rectify the situation. She probably feels better about herself than when reminded about all the times it happened in the past. And that leaves her with more willingness and emotional capacity to cooperate with you. Both of you benefit. Of course it's only human to get sick of saying the same thing for the hundredth time. That's a somewhat different problem from the shoes in the hallway. You can make good use of I-messages and explain how you feel when you experience the same problem over and over again.

Criticism "for the child's own good"?

In case you like to ponder aspects of child rearing, here's a tough topic: what is "constructive criticism"? I'm thinking about those sorts of comments we make to children with a remark like, "I'm just telling you for your own good" or "If I don't tell you, nobody else will." Do we parents have an obligation to tell our children what's "wrong" with them? Do we have the right to do so? It's worth looking deep into our selves and our motivations when we want to offer "constructive criticism."

Examples for practice

If you need some ideas for describing emotions when you're working on the examples below, you can refer back to the list on page 67.

For purposes of these exercises, we're assuming that your child starts out in the problem-free area, but that you are bothered by something. Try coming up with some really clear I-messages.

1. You've just realized that you have to do some urgent office work at home, and you told your daughter you'd drive her to riding lessons.

   ....

2. Nobody has taken the trash out even though you've asked many times.

   ....

3. Dinner is on the table and you've called the kids but they keep on playing.

   ....

4. You're concerned about your father (who is seriously ill).

   ....

5. It's past bedtime for the kids, and they're getting wilder by the minute.

   ....

6. Your teenager has stolen from the local stationery store.

   ....

I don't know how these conversations might go, or whether you would have feelings similar to mine, but here are some of my ideas as to how a parent could begin by using I-messages:

1. "Oh no! I totally forgot that I have some urgent paperwork to do this afternoon. ♞ Now I'm concerned, ♥ because I'm not sure how I can do that and take you to riding, too." ⚔

2. "I've asked you kids three times to please take out the trash. ♞ Now I'm getting really frustrated. ♥ Besides, it's in my way here." ⚔

3. "Hey, guys – dinner's getting cold! ⚔ I'd be glad ♥ if you'd come right away when I call you." ♞

4. "Listen, I'm having trouble being patient right now. ♥ I'm worried ♥ about Grandpa. You know he's been pretty sick." ♞

5. "It's bedtime. ♞ I'm concerned ♥ that you'll be tired tomorrow morning. And I need less action here so Mom and I can talk." ⚔

6. "I'm embarrassed ♥ and disappointed ♥ that you stole!" ♞

Individual and situational factors

There are certain basic requirements that need to be met in order for I-messages to work well. I'll group them into the same three categories – *parent*, *child*, and *situation* – that I use with supportive understanding:

important for the parent:
    Are you interested in talking to the child about your problem?

important for the child:
    Is he interested in listening right now?
    Is he in the no-problem zone himself?
    – or –
    Is he willing and able to listen anyhow?

important about the situation:
      Is the setting appropriate?

Practicing on your own

Try to use this way of communicating whenever you notice that you're troubled by something. At the end of this chapter there's another copy of the chart provided in Chapter 7. As you've seen by now, the important elements in I-messages are the same as those in supportive understanding: think about the video camera, the heart, and the arrows. They refer, in each case, to whichever person has the problem. Again, use the one-page chart for one "session," which can involve several exchanges between you and your child.

Very young children

What about using I-messages with kids who are too young to understand what you're saying? As with supportive understanding, the nonverbal parts of your message carry the bulk of the information. When a baby grabs for your glasses and you react by taking them off, the baby learns that you don't want your glasses grabbed. When a toddler pulls your hair and you react with a genuine "Ouch! That hurts Mommy!" then the idea gets across. Those are clear I-messages.

Time well spent

You may be wondering how time-intensive this method of communicating is. As with supportive understanding, I-messages do take more time than communicating in less constructive ways – but again, only short-term. Long-term, when you deal with challenges this way, you tend not to have the "same old problems" coming up over and over again, so you actually save time in the end. (It's like making a deposit into your savings account. Sure, it's a sacrifice at the time, but in the long run you have more for your money.) You're investing in your child's ability to respect other individuals. And you're investing in the relationship you have with your child.

Anger

Remember our discussion about anger? This is just a reminder to try looking for other emotions that may be lurking beneath the surface. An interesting thing about anger is that it's often directed toward the "other person." Focusing on anger and blame is often easier than facing one's own emotions, like fear, embarrassment, or frustration. It's more difficult to look closely at oneself. I-messages are a skill for a lifetime. Just try your best, and you'll keep on improving.

Emergencies

Just as with supportive understanding, there are times when it's more important to take action than to talk, as when your child's safety is in jeopardy. But even in such a situation, a very clear I-message after the fact can convey your feelings. "I was scared to death when I saw you running into the street where that car was driving!" communicates exactly how you felt.

Other ways to practice

Besides practicing with your child, try practicing I-messages by role playing with your partner or a friend who's interested in learning this skill. As described in Chapter 7, you can use a rope (or simply vary the distance between the two of you) to show how well understood you feel when using I-messages. This gives a good indication as to how the exercise is going.

Words of wisdom

Here are some suggestions that have helped me:

Firstly, I've discovered that my children are much more willing to listen to me when I ask them, "Are you interested in hearing what I think (or how I feel)?" before I launch into anything. That way they have the choice of saying yes or no, and they almost always say yes.

Secondly, when constructing an I-message keep it short and sweet! Children usually focus better when the message is simple. I sometimes catch myself going on and on with explanations, only to realize that my kids have tuned me out.

Thirdly, I've realized that it's often possible to use a positive I-message even when I'm having a problem. Recently I was trying to concentrate on writing, and one of my sons was concentrating just as hard – on making noise at the top of his lungs. I tried an experiment, saying to him, "You know what? I'm really proud of you when you remember to keep your voice down low enough that I can concentrate on my work." He nodded, looking surprised. Later on, when the volume increased again and I looked over in his direction, he said, "Oh, yeah – that's right!" then turned to his brother, grinning, and said, "Mommy's really proud of me when I remember to be quieter!" I don't always have the patience or foresight to be so exemplary, but it does work well when I manage it!

The matrix

Let's fill in another section of the matrix, as we've done when completing the two previous sections. In the zone where we have a problem, our responsibility as parents is to express our own needs clearly.

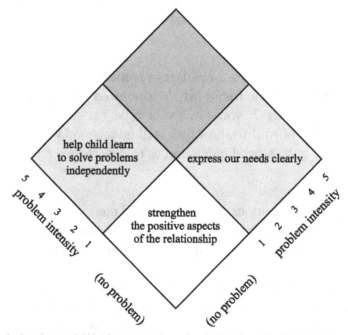

how bothered is my child by this situation?   how bothered am I by this situation?

In the next section we'll work in the red zone, where both you and your child are having problems.

Work Sheet: **I-messages when I have a problem**

date:

	situation:	result (feelings):	result (practical):

what I said:

child's reaction:

what I said:

child's reaction:

what I said:

child's reaction:

what I said:

child's reaction:

...

...

...

...

results, changes, etc.:

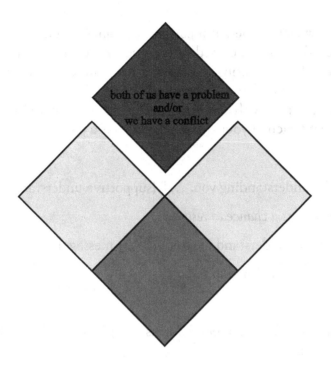

HOW TO RESOLVE MUTUAL PROBLEMS

---

10. HOW TO DEAL WITH CONFLICTS CONSTRUCTIVELY

This is it! This is the part you've been waiting for since you picked up the book. But guess what – you already have the skills you need to work constructively with conflict situations! Dealing with the red zone will be a composite of everything else you've learned so far. The only new idea is that you'll need to juggle the use of supportive understanding and I-messages, depending on what's needed at a particular moment. You'll switch back and forth between the skills you used in the two yellow areas of the matrix. It's like being in a play and acting the parts of two different characters. Let's say one character is a giant ear and the other one is a giant mouth. In the "play," both of them interact with the other person who's involved in the conflict (your child), and each of your two characters has a particular role to play:

↺ "Just so I'm understanding you: ... " (supportive understanding)

then the child has a chance to respond

⌣ "I want you to understand me, too: ... " (I-message)

then the child has a chance to respond

This type of pattern then repeats for as long as needed. Maybe the next sequence looks more like this:

↺ "So when ... happens, you feel like ... " (supportive understanding)

then the child has a chance to respond

⌣ "And my problem is that when ... happens, I feel like ... " (I-message)

then the child has a chance to respond

It's important to keep playing the role of the ear (using supportive understanding) until your child feels understood. Only then will he have the capacity and willingness to listen to your view of things. Then you can switch to playing the role of the mouth (using I-messages). That's when you have the chance to talk about *your* view of the situation. In a moment we'll have a closer look at how this works.

In this section, since you're trying to solve conflicts, the idea is to move from this:

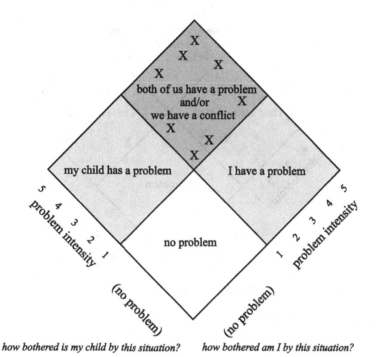

how bothered is my child by this situation?   *how bothered am I by this situation?*

with detours through the yellow areas, where both people are addressing their respective problems:

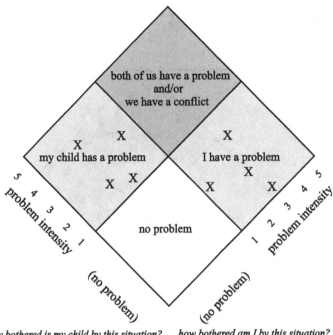

how bothered is my child by this situation?   how bothered am I by this situation?

toward this:

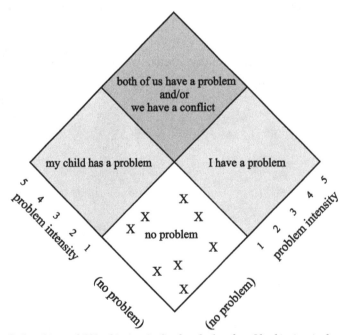

how bothered is my child by this situation?   how bothered am I by this situation?

This is a very different result from some other methods of dealing with conflicts. In families where the parents tend to be authoritarian in their approach, and the children aren't given a fair say, the parents might end up solving their own problems but the children remain in the yellow area. On the other hand, there are families in which the parents are very permissive. The children get what they want, but then the parents' needs aren't met so they remain in the yellow area.

In this section I won't repeat the guidelines about how to formulate statements of supportive understanding and I-messages. My purpose in using the same structure for those two sections of the book, with repetition of certain ideas, was to show that supportive understanding and I-messages are two sides of the same coin. You won't see the symbols (camera, heart, and arrows), either. I hope that by now you're very familiar with the elements they represent. At this stage I'd like you to concentrate on the type of message being given – supportive understanding or I-message – and see how you can switch back and forth between them most effectively.

How not to solve conflicts

Imagine a situation in which a seven-year-old doesn't want to eat his salad. The parent, of course, wants him to eat it. There's a conflict of interests. There are many less-than-ideal ways of approaching this problem. Some of them are listed below. Imagine someone saying each of these things to you (maybe even say them to yourself in the mirror), then write down your reactions.

remark:	my reactions:
You're so stubborn!	....
You'll never grow up to be a big boy.	....
No salad, no dessert!	....
I have an idea: just think about something else.	....
You have ten minutes, then watch out!	....
You always take too long eating.	....

I'm going to tell Daddy when he comes home. ....

You drive me crazy! ....

You're making me run out of patience. ....

Eat it up now, or else! ....

You should eat healthier food and less junk. ....

What's the big deal, anyhow? Just eat! ....

I'm sure you'd find room for ice cream. ....

How to do it better

Chances are, none of the remarks above made you feel good. How could the parent have begun talking about the conflict in a more constructive way? Here are some ideas as to how to begin a discussion. Again, imagine hearing these statements being made in a non-blaming way and take note of how you feel.

remark: my reactions:

You've eaten very little salad. ....

I'm wondering if you like the salad. ....

Most of the salad is still on your plate. ....

You ate up all your noodles. ....

It looks as if you liked the noodles. ....

These remarks show supportive understanding. The child has a chance to respond without feeling criticized, threatened, or backed into a corner. He probably answers with something like "Yeah, this salad tastes terrible!" or "At least the noodles are real food!" In an ideal situation, the mother is able to continue using supportive understanding until the child feels understood.

106

But that doesn't solve the problem of the mother wanting the child to eat salad, and the child not wanting to do so. Their interests are still in conflict with each other. Here are some possibilities the mother could then use to communicate her thoughts and feelings to the child. See how you'd feel if you heard these statements.

remark:	my reactions:

∽ I'd like to tell you what I think about this.

    (Are you interested?) ....

∽ I would like you to eat your salad. ....

∽ I'd like to tell you why it's good to eat salad.

    (Should I?) ....

∽ I want you to stay healthy. ....

∽ I like to take good care of you. ....

∽ I like to give you food that helps you grow up to be big and strong.

....

∽ I feel disappointed when I prepare food and then you don't eat it.

....

These remarks are I-messages. They let the child know clearly where the mother stands on the topic. The mother is maximizing the chances that her child will listen to her opinions. Of course, there's no guarantee, but this approach usually works well. When both of them understand one another, it's time to think about a practical solution to the disagreement if nothing has come up spontaneously. There are many good ways to proceed. In Appendix 1 you can read about several possibilities.

Here is an example of how the discussion about eating salad might have looked under better circumstances:

Mother: ꜱ I notice the salad is still there on your plate.

Child: Yeah, I hate salad! I'm not eating it.

Mother: ↻ You like other foods better.

Child: At least the noodles tasted good.

Mother: ↻ Well, I can understand that you'd rather eat noodles.

Child: Right!

Mother: Would you like to hear what I think?

Child: All right …

Mother: ⌣ I like to see you eat food that helps you stay healthy.

Child: Hm.

Mother: ⌣ I'd be glad if you ate some of the salad.

Child: How about if I eat half of it – would *that* make you happy?

Mother: ⌣ I really like that idea!

You may be thinking to yourself that things just don't work this well in real life. And sometimes they don't. You'll be amazed, though, how often they do. What a concept – treating kids with such respect! Children are usually raised to respect their parents and other adults. You'll be surprised how cooperative and reasonable children are when they're treated that way, too. When I'm short on patience, I try to ask myself whether I'd be talking to a friend the same way I'm talking to my child right now. That can be a sobering experience.

Here's one more example of a problem-solving session where each party ends up feeling better and understanding the other one a bit more:

Child: Why are you talking to me in such an angry voice? I didn't do

                anything bad!

Mother: ↻ You don't like me to talk that way to you.

⌣ I'm sorry. I know you didn't do anything wrong. I'm just annoyed with your sister, so I guess that affects my whole mood right now.

Child: I still don't think it's fair to me, though.

Mother: ◠ I understand how you feel when I do that.

⌣ I'm glad you let me know how you're feeling!

Examples for practice

Try coming up with an appealing supportive listening statement and a clear I-message for each of these examples.

1. Daughter refuses to stop playing and clean up; guests are about to arrive.

   ◠ ....

   ⌣ ....

2. Teenager doesn't want to go on vacation with the family but parents aren't willing to let her stay home alone.

   ◠ ....

   ⌣ ....

3. Children are hungry and mother doesn't feel like cooking yet.

   ◠ ....

   ⌣ ....

4. Child wants to keep watching TV but it's bedtime.

   ◠ ....

⌣ ....

5. Child keeps getting up out of bed; parents want time to themselves.

𝒥 ....

⌣ ....

6. Children are arguing and being physically aggressive with each other.

𝒥 ....

⌣ ....

Here are some of my ideas for supportive understanding and I-messages:

1. 𝒥 You'd really rather keep on playing right now than clean up.
   ⌣ I'd like to have the living room cleaned up before our guests arrive.

2. 𝒥 I understand that it would be more fun for you to stay here and be able to see your friends than to go on vacation with us.
   ⌣ I'd be worried about you being in the house alone when we're so far away.

3. 𝒥 You kids are really hungry and want to eat right this minute!
   ⌣ I'd just like to finish reading this one page before I get the food.

4. 𝒥 That TV program is so entertaining.
   ⌣ I want you to be well rested tomorrow morning.

5. 𝒥 You seem to be having trouble getting to sleep.

⌣ Mommy and Daddy would really like some time to ourselves.

6. ☺ You two are furious with one another!

⌣ I'm afraid someone's going to get hurt!

Practicing on your own

Keeping your roles straight

Sometimes it's a real challenge to keep track of which "role" you're playing when working through a conflict. The more clarity you have as to whether you're paying attention to the other person (with supportive understanding) or whether you're explaining your own position (with I-messages), the more constructive the process becomes. To help you maintain clarity, there's a page at the end of this section with a giant ear and a giant mouth on it. Make a copy of it and cut the copy in two. Whenever you're working through a conflict, be sure you're holding up one or the other picture (but not both!) at any given point in time. That way it's clear to you whether you're using supportive understanding or an I-message. Children really like to do this, too, and sometimes want to have their own sets of pictures.

More than two people

If three or more people are involved in a conflict, of course it's a bit more complicated. Try to break down the situation into pieces you can handle. Use supportive understanding with one child at a time, for instance, until each one feels he's being understood. Then talk about your own position in the conflict when the others can listen.

Children in conflict with one another

Sometimes your children are having a problem with one another and need your help, even though you're not otherwise involved in the problem (you're in the green zone). Use supportive understanding with each child in turn. That helps the children understand both themselves and the other child better. It's like being a translator and mediator who says to one child, "So – what I'm understanding from you is that when ... happens, you feel like ..." You then turn to the other child and say something like, "I just want to make sure you understand that, too. Can you imagine how your sister is feeling?"

Of course this kind of situation can take you, as a parent, out of the green zone. Then you need to decide at each point along the way which method of talking to the children (with supportive understanding or I-messages) is most constructive at that moment.

Avoiding the heat of the moment

It's often more productive to deal with conflicts when you're not in the midst of one. That way, emotions are less in the foreground and it's easier to concentrate on finding ways to avoid the conflict in the future. Find a time when there are no shoes strewn around in the hallway, and your kids aren't in the midst of an uninterruptible activity. Then you can say, "Hey, when I'm walking in with groceries and there are shoes lying around on the floor, it's a real problem for me. I'm afraid I'll trip. How can we keep that from happening?" You'll get more cooperation and creative suggestions from them than when the problem has already materialized.

No conflict, just simultaneous problems

If you find yourself in the red zone (where both you and the other person are having problems), there isn't necessarily a conflict between the two of you. Maybe you've had a tough day at work, and your child is unhappy about something that happened in school. It's a delicate matter, then, of finding the right balance between paying attention to your child and taking care of yourself. You need to do some juggling between supportive understanding and I-messages to find the balance that works for both of you at that particular moment. As you can imagine, though, these types of situations can turn very easily into conflicts, since people are more sensitive when something is already bothering them. But now you have a wonderful set of skills to minimize the chances of that happening!

Conflicts can be frightening

I know many adults who find it difficult to face conflicts. It's often a very new experience to talk about one's own feelings clearly in a situation where there are strong and uncomfortable emotions on both sides. Just try going at your own speed. Your children will be glad that you're being more open. As one 47-year-old woman wrote, when thinking back on her childhood, "I'd like to have had open and honest talks with my mother, but she always withdrew from conflict situations. And I'd like to have had a father that I could really discuss things with and argue with in a fair way!"

When your child experiences your increasing comfort with these new ways of interacting, she'll start to become more at ease, too. One mother explained happily at the end of our parenting class that her shy fourteen-year-old daughter had become much more courageous about broaching difficult topics and working out conflicts.

Keep in mind that the people and the relationships are more important than the particulars of the problems or exactly how you go about trying to solve them.

When there's no agreement in sight

Sometimes it seems as though you're getting nowhere in working out a disagreement. There's almost always something that you *can* agree on, though, like postponing the discussion, getting help from a third party, or working out a part of the problem at a time, for example. As I mentioned in previous sections, it helps to concentrate clearly on the "here and now," instead of bringing up similar situations from the past. That way, the current difficulties seem less overwhelming.

As one of my sons pointed out to me upon reading this manuscript, a conflict can be a good opportunity to work toward the common goal of solving the problem together. If you look far enough, you can locate common interests among warring parties, otherwise they wouldn't be involved in the problem together. The trick is being motivated to find a solution that's good for everyone, rather than concentrating on proving yourself "right" and the other person "wrong." We all want to end up in the green area.

The matrix

Now we can fill in the last section of the matrix. In this zone, our responsibility as parents is to solve conflicts as constructively as possible.

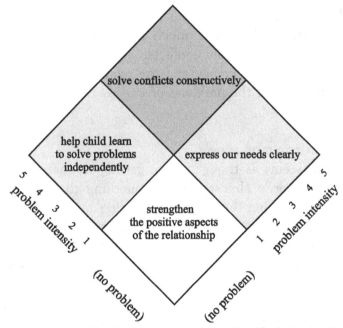

how bothered is my child by this situation?   how bothered am I by this situation?

Following is a slightly different chart for recording your problem-solving sessions. In addition to jotting down the important elements of what you've said, as in the previous charts, there's space for indicating whether your statement was an example of supportive understanding (an ear is pictured) or an I-message (there's a mouth). Have fun, and good luck!

Work Sheet: **Supportive Understanding and I-messages during conflicts**

date:

type of message	situation:	result: (feelings)	result: (practical)
⊃ or ‿	♟	♥	✗

what I said:

child's reaction:

what I said:

child's reaction:

what I said:

child's reaction:

what I said:

child's reaction:

…

…

…

…

results, changes, etc.:

CONCLUSION: THE END OF THE BEGINNING

The matrix

We can view the communications matrix in a different way that was pointed out to me by a client of mine who is an engineer. If we split the matrix down the middle, we can look at the left half as the "supportive understanding area," and the right half as the "I-messages area." Just for variety, have a look from this viewpoint:

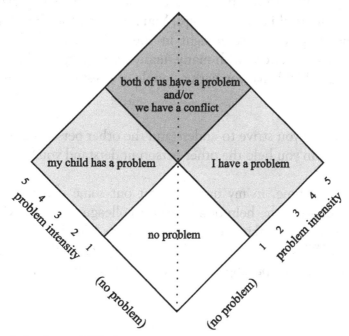

how bothered is my child by this situation?   how bothered am I by this situation?

It's a process

In my work with parents, I see over and over again that people absorb this information about communication at whatever speed and whatever depth are appropriate for them at that particular time. It depends on where they are in the whole process. For that reason, it can be very helpful to pick up this book again later, maybe a few months from now. You'll absorb the information differently compared to the first time. Besides, reminders are useful when you're learning new skills. Best of all, you'll see how far you've progressed since your first reading. I'm very interested in your personal stories. You can go to www.communication-crystal-clear.com to contact me.

So where do you go from here?

You've already come a long way, parents! I hope by this point you've found ways to integrate the material of this book into your everyday life. These are skills to treasure and develop for the rest of your days. Maybe you've realized, too, that the skills we've practiced are as valuable in other relationships as they are in parent-child relationships. You now have the chance to make the world a better place, starting right in your own family and expanding to include your interactions with many, many other people. Make the most of what you know! I'll leave you with a couple of questions you can use on your journey:

> How can you strive to understand the other person better?
> How can you help the other person understand you better?

From time to time, in my quest to sort out some complex child-rearing issues, I've enlisted the help of a therapist colleague of mine who has many years of experience working with children. Once, when I felt at my wits' end, I asked her, "Why *me*?" She looked at me wisely and said, "Because *you* can do it!" And that's my parting message to you: You can do it, too!

APPENDIX 1. PRACTICAL PROBLEM-SOLVING METHODS

After you've used supportive understanding with your child and think she's moving on to the actual problem-solving stage, it's a good idea to check whether your impression is correct. You can continue using supportive understanding and say something like, "So now it sounds as though you're wondering just *how* you'd like to deal with that situation." Then, when the emotional components are no longer in the forefront, we need some practical ideas for finding solutions. In this section are a few methods that I've found useful.

"6-step" method

This is a widely used procedure for gathering many ideas in a nonjudgmental manner. It lends itself well to being used in families and other groups.

1. Define the conflict or goal
This step ensures that all people involved understand and agree on what it is they want to accomplish. The problem doesn't necessarily involve a conflict. Maybe there's a common problem and people are cooperating to find a solution. (A conflict can be viewed this way, too, if you consider that everyone has the common goal of solving the conflict.) Example: the family is trying to decide where to go on vacation.

2. Brainstorm
The idea here is to gather as many ideas as possible without evaluating the ideas as to their usefulness or practicality. Eliminate comments like "Oh, that can't work because ..." to foster creativity. Children often come up with wonderful ideas if they're encouraged to do so. "I think we should get a rocket ship and fly to the moon!" may not be the final solution, but it's great when a four-year-old can contribute to a serious family discussion.

3. Evaluate
Here's where the individual suggestions are screened for usefulness. You can put your communications skills to work well during this phase, so as to keep

the discussion constructive. "I'd love to be able to do that – what an idea! It's a shame that's too expensive for us this year."

4. *Decide*
Now a decision is made as to which suggestion seems as if it will work the best. "Okay, so we agree that spending a week at the beach would be the best option this year."

5. *Implement*
In this phase, decisions are made as to who does what, when, how, and so forth. "I'll call the kennel this week to make sure there's space for the dog."

6. *Follow up after the fact*
Is everything moving along as planned, or are there more points to clarify, more assignments to agree upon, and so on?

Open-ended questions

There are many types of questions you can use to nudge your child in the direction of coming up with ideas. Here are a few possibilities out of many:

1. *What will be different when you've solved this problem?*
This helps children get clear on exactly what their goals are (like looking fantastic at the party, as opposed to having to wear a particular pair of jeans).

2. *What would (best friend, idol, etc.) do in that situation?*
This is useful for looking at a problem from different perspectives.

3. *What's worked before in similar situations?*
Children realize that they've been successful in the past, and that they have problem-solving skills.

4. *I wonder what might happen if you tried doing … ?*
Children can play out various possibilities in their imagination before actually making decisions.

5. Let's make believe you're (person x) and I'll make believe I'm you. We can try out different solutions and see what happens.
This is a great way to look at things from different vantage points and play through different scenarios.

6. What could make this less of a problem for you?
Especially in situations that are hard to avoid (like going to school or getting inoculations), this is a good way for a child to experience some measure of control over what's happening.

7. What would you do if you wanted to make the problem much, much worse?
This is one of my favorites, because it can be so much fun. Children always have answers to that question. And if they know how to make the situation worse, they almost always know, by deduction, how to make it better.

APPENDIX 2. QUESTIONS PEOPLE OFTEN ASK

What's really new about this book?
This new way of looking at problem situations will lead you to an intuitive understanding of what goes wrong between parents and children, and why. There are clear guidelines about which communications skills to use (and when), with step by step instructions for doing so. It's like the difference between having a pile of building blocks and having a recognizable structure made out of those blocks.

Isn't it artificial to use a theoretical approach when dealing with my own children?
Yes, theory is always different from practice, and when everything hums along happily, we don't usually worry about theory. But when difficulties pop up, that's exactly the time that a theoretical structure helps us find clarity. Then it's much easier to deal with the particulars of the real situation. It's like learning in driver training that when you're driving twice as fast you need four times the distance to stop, instead of making the discovery for yourself at an inopportune moment.

Is this a cure-all for problems between parents and kids?
No, but it comes closer than anything else I've seen so far!

Doesn't this approach take up too much time?
These methods are initially time-consuming, but will save you time and spare you problems in the longer run. It's similar to taking the time to make a list before you go shopping. That saves time in the store and minimizes the chances of having to go back again and again to get what you need.

What about really young children, or those with special needs? What about cultural or gender differences?
These ways of interacting are adaptable to all ages and all sorts of situations. It's a matter of varying the basic skills to accommodate particular needs. Respect for the child is the common denominator.

What if my partner doesn't use the skills described in this book?
They will still work for you and your child. Besides, people learn and absorb a lot by example, so your partner may move in the same direction when you're least expecting it.

Why encourage kids to think about "negative" feelings?
Paradoxically, dealing supportively with unpleasant feelings is the best way of helping a child move through them and on to a more enjoyable existence.

Is it okay to interact differently with different children?
Yes, children are separate individuals with differing needs and characteristics. In addition, each child brings out different characteristics in us as parents. When my sisters and I compare notes about our childhoods, it often seems that we must have had entirely different sets of parents!

Can I use these ways of communicating with my partner? friends? colleagues?
Yes, yes, yes! Please do. See my website at www.communication-crystal-clear.com for additional publications and support I offer in other areas.

So how do I proceed from here, now that I've read the book and done the exercises?
These are skills for a lifetime. That means that you can keep on working on them and improving forever. (No matter how many sessions my courses include, participants tell me they want more!)

It's beneficial, too, to get together with other parents to work through concrete situations where things didn't go as well as you had hoped. Rereading the book at some later point can be very helpful, because you'll absorb the information differently when you have experience behind you. If you want information direct from the source, have a look at my website for news and free tips, or email me with your questions.

I've tried my best, but I still have trouble with certain of these new skills. What should I do?
You can join our forum (see my website for information) or send me an email with your questions.

What can I do when nothing works between my kids and me?
Besides seeking out support in a peer group or from a counselor, you can email me to arrange for a personal consultation.

What else should I read on this topic?
Rather than making specific recommendations, since I don't know you or your needs, how about browsing through the appropriate sections of a bookstore? You can do so in a real store or electronically. When I do that, I usually find that certain books jump out at me, according to what I'm particularly interested in and what I need right then. In addition, it's worth looking at books that have to do with good self-care, like nutrition and exercise. I know that the better care I take of myself, the better care I can take of other people.

APPENDIX 3. SURVEY RESULTS: CHILDREN RATE PARENTS

This small survey (27 teenagers and 16 adults) addressed the quality of current relationships between eleventh-graders and their parents, and between adults and their parents, in retrospect, with those adults reflecting back on their childhoods. My goal was to gather some information from individuals with whom I had no work connections. This was not intended to be a large-scale scientific study.

Sixteen statements were listed (see next two pages) with a numerical range for answers. In addition, each participant was asked what was best about the parent, and what he would like the parent to have done differently. The survey was conducted in writing and was anonymous, except for gender and age. Each participant filled in a separate form for mother and father.

In case you'd like to fill out the survey yourself before looking at my results, you can use the forms on the next two pages, one to rate your mother and one to rate your father. The scale goes from zero to ten, with zero being the worst possible rating and ten being the best.

My survey results appear on the last two pages. Chart 1 shows the ratings given by the teenagers to their parents; Chart 2 shows the ratings given by the adult participants to their parents. In both charts, ratings are shown for each gender combination (for example, girls rating their mothers). The average rating for each gender combination is also indicated.

In both groups the relationships between fathers and daughters were rated the most poorly. In both groups mothers were rated more favorably than fathers by both daughters and sons.

mother

(worst)										(best)
0	1	2	3	4	5	6	7	8	9	10

rating:

1. My mother had enough time for me. ....

2. My mother was interested in me and my life. ....

3. I could rely on my mother. ....

4. My mother treated me with respect. ....

5. My mother valued my opinions. ....

6. My mother was a good role model. ....

7. My mother was open and honest. ....

8. I got enough support from my mother. ....

9. I could talk to my mother about my feelings. ....

10. My mother respected my privacy. ....

11. She gave me the right amount of responsibility and freedom. ....

12. The atmosphere was good when my mother was around. ....

13. I was intellectually and culturally supported by my mother. ....

14. My mother valued physical health (nutrition, exercise, attitude toward drugs, etc.). ....

15. My mother loved me. ....

16. My mother accepted me the way I was. ....

father

(worst)										(best)
0	1	2	3	4	5	6	7	8	9	10

rating:

1. My father had enough time for me.   ....

2. My father was interested in me and my life.   ....

3. I could rely on my father.   ....

4. My father treated me with respect.   ....

5. My father valued my opinions.   ....

6. My father was a good role model.   ....

7. My father was open and honest.   ....

8. I got enough support from my father.   ....

9. I could talk to my father about my feelings.   ....

10. My father respected my privacy.   ....

11. He gave me the right amount of responsibility and freedom.   ....

12. The atmosphere was good when my father was around.   ....

13. I was intellectually and culturally supported by my father.   ....

14. My father valued physical health (nutrition, exercise,

    attitude toward drugs, etc.).   ....

15. My father loved me.   ....

16. My father accepted me the way I was.   ....

CHART 1: teenagers rate their fathers and mothers

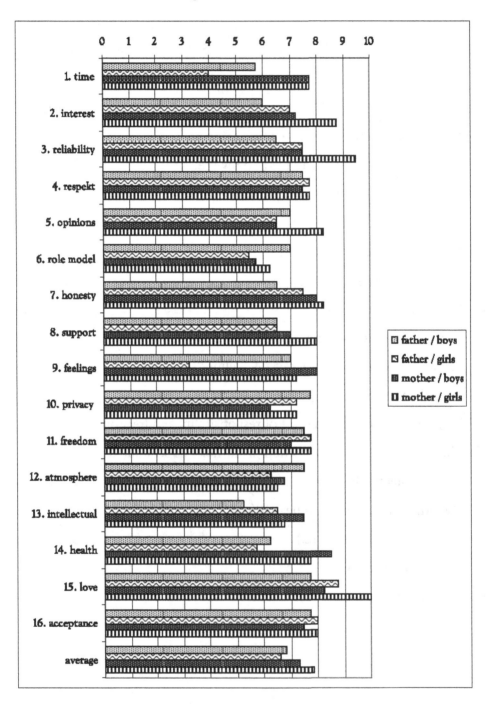

CHART 2: adults rate their fathers and mothers

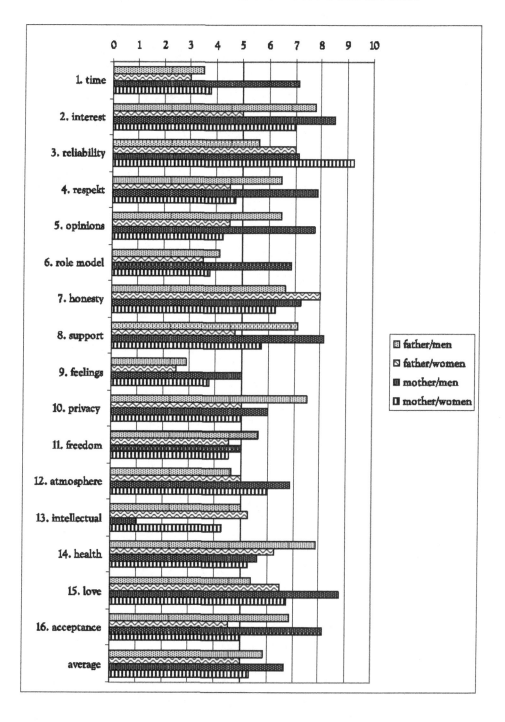

NOTES

NOTES

NOTES

NOTES

.

NOTES

Printed in the United States
By Bookmasters